PERSONAL CYBERSECURITY
MANUAL

How Anyone Can Protect Themselves from
Fraud, Identity Theft, and *Other Cybercrimes*

MARLON BUCHANAN

HomeTechHacker.com

ISBN: 978-1-958648-00-1 (paperback)
ISBN: 978-1-958648-01-8 (ebook)
ISBN: 978-1-958648-02-5 (audiobook)

Edited by Graham Southorn

Dedication and Acknowledgements

The journey to being a published non-fiction author has been a challenge. I would not be publishing my fourth book without the encouragement of my family, my friends, and others, who have supported me. I'd like to thank them all.

I'd like to dedicate this book to everyone, strangers and acquaintances alike, who have sent me a kind word about one of my previous books. I write these books to help people, and knowing that I am is what keeps me going. Your encouragement means the world to me.

Other Books by Marlon Buchanan

- *The Home Network Manual: The Complete Guide to Setting Up, Upgrading, and Securing Your Home Network*
- *The Smart Home Manual: How to Automate Your Home to Keep Your Family Entertained, Comfortable, and Safe*
- *Home Wi-Fi Tuneup: Practical Steps You Can Take to Speed Up, Stabilize, and Secure Your Home Wi-Fi*

All books are available in Kindle and paperback formats. The *Home Network Manual* and *The Smart Home Manual* are also available as audiobooks. You can learn more about these books, including where to buy them, at MarlonBuchanan.com.

Subscribe to HomeTechHacker.com

Be sure to check out HomeTechHacker.com for free in-depth articles about cybersecurity, home networks, smart homes, and more. In addition to the articles, you'll find the following free resources:

- **HomeTechHacker Technology Advisor** — Need personalized advice for home technology purchases? This tool will ask you a few questions and recommend technology specific to your needs.
- **HomeTechHacker Wi-Fi Guide** — Following this guide will ensure you have fast, stable, and secure Wi-Fi throughout your home.
- **HomeTechHacker Resource Bundle** — This free resource bundle is filled with checklists and links to online resources to help you make the most of your home tech.
- **HomeTechHacker Technology Personality Quizzes** — Take fun personality quizzes that will entertain you, inform you, and maybe you will learn something about yourself.
- **Email Courses** — Interested in building a smart home and don't know where to start? Are you worried about your home network security? Sign up for these free courses to make your home smart and secure your home network in 5 days!

Also, subscribe to my newsletter to get the latest updates about cybersecurity and other home technology topics.

Contents

PART 3: Protecting Your Home Network

PART 4: Special Considerations for Older People and Children

PART 5: The Future of Cybersecurity

Preface

The technology in the world we live in is amazing. The phenomenal pace at which the online world has progressed this century has reshaped our lives. Think about all the things you can do online now! You can apply to college, get a job, and buy almost anything you want right from a home computer or a mobile device anywhere in the world. You can communicate with your friends and family and even thousands of strangers instantly through social media. Young people growing up now can't even remember a world where this technology and connectedness didn't exist.

These wonderful abilities to transact and to share online aren't without their pitfalls. Criminals follow opportunities, and these technologies have created new ways for them to commit crimes. For example, I once had packages stolen from my porch. Luckily, I was able to use footage from my surveillance cameras to help the police track down the thieves. These cameras help me know who is at my door and when packages have been delivered. Unfortunately, they can also be hacked to spy on me. These days, I worry more about my cameras being hacked than my packages being stolen.

My family keeps cherished home photos and videos, key financial documentation, and other important files on a network-attached storage device (NAS). Our NAS provides reliable storage, but it's vulnerable to hackers. All major NAS brands have been the target of multiple ransomware attacks, including mine.

These types of attacks have just added to the types of personal cybersecurity issues we already have to be aware of. Thieves still pilfer mail in hopes to find something that can help steal your identity. Scammers still con people into giving away personal details and credit card information over the phone and through email.

You can do a great job of securing your home network and not falling prey to scammers, and still be a cybersecurity victim. The problem is that you don't have control over the way others protect your private data. Large companies like Home Depot, Facebook, and Marriott have all leaked private data to hackers.

I've painted a dire picture, but you can protect yourself. You can stop hackers from breaking into your home network. You can learn practices to prevent your accounts from being compromised. You can take proactive steps to protect your identity, even if a company leaks your private data. Good personal cybersecurity practices will only grow in importance as technology advances. This book gives you all the tools you need to protect yourself.

About This Book

■ Whom Is This Book for?

Ransomware, spyware, phishing, viruses, credit card fraud, identity theft, compromised passwords... Either you think about some of these terms and worry, or you don't think about them but should be. According to the Insurance Information Institute, identity theft and fraud reports have grown 56 percent between 2016 and 2020. Cybercrimes were up 165 percent during the same period. Additionally, the number of data breaches grew by 137 percent between 2015 and 2021.[1] Cybercrimes are on the rise, and we must do all we can to educate and protect ourselves.

We live in the world where our lives are conducted online more and more. Your home network may have computers, mobile and streaming devices, smart speakers, and other gadgets. You probably have online accounts at banks; social media sites; email, healthcare and many other service providers. The average person has over one hundred

---

[1] "Facts + Statistics: Identity Theft and Cybercrime," Insurance Information Institute, accessed August 23, 2022, https://www.iii.org/fact-statistic/facts-statistics-identity-theft-and-cybercrime.

online accounts! Each one of these accounts contains your private data — addresses, date of birth, Social Security numbers, financial information, and maybe even your children's information.

With all this information available on our home networks and online, we all have to take extra steps to protect ourselves.

Do you want to know how to protect your home network from hackers? Are you worried about bad actors breaking into your online accounts and committing identity fraud? Would you like to educate yourself about cybercrimes, your vulnerabilities, and ways to protect yourself and your family? If any of these things are true, this book is for you.

When you are done reading this book, you'll know the following:

- Different types of cybersecurity attacks
- Ways to protect your devices, yourself, and your family from online and offline attacks
- Best practices for protecting your online accounts from unauthorized access
- Ways to secure your home network from hackers
- What to do if your accounts, devices, or identity are compromised
- Ways to counter attacks specifically targeted towards older adults and young children

You don't need any particular background to understand or benefit from this book. You have enough knowledge to benefit from this book if you have any online accounts or use any online services. You can especially benefit from this book if you are responsible for configuring your, or someone else's, home network. If you have any type of electronic footprint (created by you or by a company), then you are ready for this book.

How to Use This Book

This book steps you through the ways of protecting yourself from cybersecurity attacks. It starts by providing a foundation of knowledge. Then, using that knowledge, the book guides you through the process of developing good cybersecurity practices. If you read this book sequentially, you'll learn about the different types of attacks; best practices for protecting yourself, your family, and your home network; and future trends in cybersecurity.

Although this book is intended to be read sequentially, it works well as a reference for those with prior knowledge who look to home in on various subjects. The layout and headings make it easy to quickly find the information you may be looking for.

Be sure to take advantage of the glossary, checklists, and additional resources in the appendix. Cybersecurity involves a lot of jargon, and the glossary is there to explain all these technical terms. The checklists give you a quick way to track your progress in accomplishing the recommendations you'll find in each chapter. Finally, the additional resources in the appendix are links to up-to-date home technology resources.

Conventions Used in This Book

Here are the conventions used in this book, which highlight important information:

- **What I Do** – In several sections of this book, I give specific information and address the discussed topics in the context of my own life. For example, in the home network security section, I discuss some of the security steps I've taken. I'm not suggesting that what I do is the best thing for everyone. Instead, these sections are intended to give you practical real-world examples of what's possible.
- **In the Real World** – Throughout the book, you'll find useful stories and case studies about cybersecurity to help connect the material in this book to real-world scenarios.
- **Key Takeaways** – At the end of each part, I provide a checklist of the key information that you can use as a summary for quick reference.

Part 1

Introduction to Cybersecurity

What Is Cybersecurity?

Cybersecurity refers to the measures taken to protect computer networks, devices, and data from unauthorized or criminal use. It's also the practice of ensuring confidentiality, integrity, and availability of information. Cybersecurity helps us safely rely on many of the technologies we use every day.

Although the term *cybersecurity* dates back to the late 1980s, the recognition of the need for cybersecurity comes from the 1970s. In 1971, Bob Thomas wrote a program called Creeper that was designed to move between mainframe computers using ARPANET (the precursor to the Internet we know and love today). Creeper wasn't particularly destructive; it just output the text "I'M THE CREEPER; CATCH ME IF YOU CAN." Roy Tomlinson, the inventor of email, later modified this program, and it became the first computer worm copying itself between computers rather than just moving from computer to computer. Roy later wrote another program called Reaper, which would chase the Creeper program and delete it. Reaper was the first antivirus software.

From those early moments of connected computers being able to infect other computers, cybercrime was born. Criminals quickly realized they could use these types of programs to maliciously steal information, take control of computers, and shut down computer systems. Early hacks included the Morris worm, which ground the Internet to a halt in 1988, and the PC Cyborg Trojan in 1989, which was the first known ransomware (a cyberattack where your computer files are encrypted and the attacker demands a ransom to unencrypt them). These types of attacks were rare back then, but they are commonplace now. Cyberattacks and the need for cybersecurity have existed for longer than most of us have been using the Internet.

This book refers to *personal cybersecurity*, which I define slightly differently from what is known as *general cybersecurity*. Most general cybersecurity practices focus on companies and other organizations' practices to protect their computer systems. I consider personal cybersecurity to be the practice of individuals and families protecting their devices, home networks, privacy, identity, and data from attacks of all kinds. Personal cybersecurity protects you from not just hackers online. It also protects your data and privacy from bad actors who will use this data both online and offline to cause you harm. In essence, my definition of personal cybersecurity adds *information security*, which means protecting and controlling access to your data wherever it is, to cybersecurity. When I use the term cybersecurity in this book, I refer to this definition of personal cybersecurity.

 ## Why Is Cybersecurity Important?

Life today often involves using lots of different devices to perform various activities online. It involves having your home and the devices in it constantly connected to the Internet. It involves many companies collecting, storing, and sometimes selling important information that they gather about you online.

Examples of this include all your activity on Facebook, YouTube, and other social media accounts; the terms you've searched for on Google and the sites you've visited; paying for merchandise online at Amazon, Walmart, and any of your favorite vendors; even online discussions and transactions with doctors, bankers, lawyers, employers, and many other organizations—all involving your most sensitive information.

Imagine if anyone could get any of this information at any time. They could impersonate you and access your money and damage your credit. They could ruin your reputation online. They could stop you from accessing the services you need. They could cost you hundreds of hours and thousands of dollars to repair the damage they've done. And trust me, people try to get at this information and use it for nefarious purposes 24 hours a day and seven days a week.

Additionally, many people have been increasing the number of attackable devices connected to their home networks. Surveillance cameras, smart speakers, smart TVs, robot vacuums, and many other devices are wonderful conveniences to have in your home. But they also increase the number of ways a cyberattack can compromise your home network.

Good cybersecurity practices are important to protect you and your family's present and future. It's paramount that you protect your devices, data, and identity in the world where you use all these things just to go about your regular life.

Why Cyberattacks Are on the Rise

The number of cyberattacks has been increasing, and that's another reason why cybersecurity is important and why you should take extra steps to protect yourself. As mentioned earlier, the cybercrime volume has risen by 165 percent from 2016 to 2020. The frequency of ransomware attacks has exploded, growing by 105 percent worldwide in 2021.[2] The trend hasn't been slowing down; it's speeding up and probably will continue for the foreseeable future. But why?

No one has definitive answers on what's leading to the increase in attacks. Cybersecurity professionals generally cite one or more of the following factors:

- An increase in the use of online services: With more online services and more people online, attackers get more opportunities.
- An increase in remote work: Companies as a whole are better at protecting their systems than home users are. Unfortunately, many of the protections companies have developed don't extend to remote workers.

---

[2] Amiah Taylor, "There's a Huge Surge in Hackers Holding Data for Ransom, and Experts Want Everyone to Take These Steps," Fortune, accessed August 23, 2022, https://fortune.com/2022/02/17/ransomware-attacks-surge-2021-report/.

More people working remotely means more prey for cybercriminals.

- The rise of cryptocurrency: Cryptocurrencies like Bitcoin (BTC) are harder to trace than other forms of payment are. This allows hackers to get paid while maintaining their anonymity.
- Victims' willingness to pay the ransom: Companies and individuals keep paying the ransom when hit by ransomware. If criminals could rob a bank, walk away with the money, and never get caught, there would probably be more bank robberies. This is what is happening with ransomware.
- Cyberattacks on countries: Cyberattacks have increasingly become a safer way to attack a country or parts of a country. In many ways, these politically motivated attacks are a new face of war.
- The availability of ransomware-as-a-service. Cybercriminals can now "lease" ransomware, significantly lowering the technological barrier to entry for ransomware crimes.

What Are the Different Types of Cyberattacks?

Cyberattacks have greatly evolved since Bob Thomas' Creeper virus. Today, there are many different types of attacks that take different approaches to their incursions. In this section, I describe the most common cyberattacks. This list is by no means comprehensive, but it encompasses the majority of cyberattacks that bad actors employ.

Figure 1. Some of the common cyberattacks explained in this section.

Viruses

A computer virus is a malicious program that can propagate itself from device to device, much like a human virus goes from human to human. The virus infects computers by changing the way they work. It can destroy files, prevent your computer from working, spy on you, and/or steal private data. A virus attaches itself to files and other programs on a computer. When that file or program is transmitted to another computer, so is the virus. This often happens through email attachments.

Worms

Even though the terms *virus* and *worm* are often used interchangeably, they aren't the same thing. A worm is a self-replicating type of virus. Unlike a basic virus, it doesn't need to attach itself to an infected file or program to move to another computer. It uses a vulnerability in a computer and/or computer network to copy itself to other computers. Thus, worms typically spread much faster than basic viruses do, because they replicate themselves.

Trojans

Trojans, or Trojan horse viruses, are another popular virus variant. Like in the famous story of the Trojan Horse from Homer's poem *The Odyssey*, this virus version masquerades as a legitimate computer program before whipping off its mask to reveal its pernicious intentions. Often, these types of viruses create a backdoor (a way for an unauthorized person to access a computer) for the attacker to exploit at their leisure.

Spyware

Spyware is software that covertly gathers data about the computer and/or the computer's users and forwards that information to an attacker or some other third party. Spyware can be used legitimately too. For example, employers may use spyware to monitor their employees' activities. Similarly, parents may do the same with their children's devices. However, malicious spyware is used to profit from stolen data.

Spyware, like viruses, can also cause other problems on your computer network. It can slow down your device and network.

Ransomware

Ransomware is a type of attack that prevents or limits users' access to their computers and/or files. The attackers then demand a ransom in order to restore full access. This is the fastest-growing type of cyberattack.

Brute-Force Attacks

These are attacks where hackers try to gain access to accounts or systems by guessing the usernames and passwords. Simple versions of this attack involve a cybercriminal typing in guessed usernames and passwords until they can successfully log in. A more sophisticated version of this attack involves a computer program using a list of words that it enters one after the other for the username and/or password.

Social Engineering

Social engineering attacks, sometimes referred to as human hacking, are attempts by hackers to trick people into giving them access, private information, or other useful data. These attacks can happen in person, by phone call, online, and via other types of interaction. Typically, an attacker will gather information about a target, try to establish some type of trust, and then influence the target into taking the attacker's desired action. This process can take place in a single email or phone call or over several months through multiple forms of communication.

Phishing

Phishing is a social engineering attack in which bad actors try to trick users into revealing personal information, such as passwords and credit card numbers, through fraudulent solicitation, usually from an email or a website. The following are some common types of phishing attacks:

- Deceptive phishing: An attacker impersonates a legitimate company, usually by setting up a fraudulent website that looks similar to that of the real company and has a similar URL, in an attempt to steal your personal information or login credentials.
- Spear phishing: A bad actor customizes the attack by using publicly available information from sources like LinkedIn and Facebook in an effort to make you think you have a connection with a real person whom you can trust. The intent is to make you also trust a link or an email attachment that will help get some of your personal data.
- Whale phishing: An attacker uses a compromised executive's email address, often a fake email address or a similar-looking address, to send an email to an employee. The intent is to get the employee to reveal personal information or to transfer company funds or sensitive information to the attacker.

Network Penetration

Network penetration is when hackers search for, and identify, security vulnerabilities in your network or on the connected computers in your network. Hackers exploit these vulnerabilities to gain access to and control of your network devices and data. There are many ways to penetrate a network, including hacking Wi-Fi signals, bypassing firewall controls, and using phishing techniques and credential hacking (i.e., using someone else's credentials without permission).

Denial-of-Service/Distributed Denial-of-Service

Denial-of-service (DoS) and distributed denial-of-service (DDoS) attacks flood a network and/or a device on the network with traffic, making that network or device unavailable. A DDoS attack is a DoS attack that uses multiple machines to attack a system. Usually, these attacking systems are in multiple locations, making it (1) more difficult to stop the attack completely and (2) easier for the attacker to take down the system.

DDoS attacks most often use computers that hackers have previously compromised (called zombies or bots) to carry out attacks coordinated by a command-and-control server. This network of connected and compromised machines carrying out the DDoS attack is called a botnet.

DNS Spoofing

Domain Name System, or DNS, is the system that assigns names to Internet Protocol (IP) addresses. Imagine having to remember 172.217.164.110 instead of google.com or 64.233.177.190 instead of youtube.com. DNS maps names to IP addresses to make services like websites much easier to remember. With DNS spoofing, attackers alter DNS records (either by intercepting them and changing them or compromising a DNS server) to send people to malicious sites instead of the intended ones. These malicious sites can then install malware and employ phishing techniques and many other attacks.

Man-in-the-Middle

A man-in-the-middle (MitM) attack, sometimes called eavesdropping, is when an attacker positions themselves in between the communications of two systems to eavesdrop and/or impersonate one of the systems while making it appear as if the two systems are communicating normally. The goal of this attack, like others, is to steal personal information such as login credentials and credit card numbers.

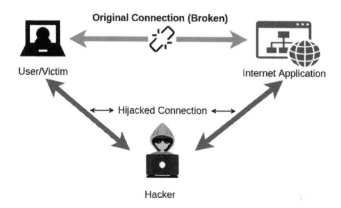

Figure 2. Diagram of a man-in-the-middle attack.

Cross-Site Scripting

Cross-site scripting (XSS) attacks occur against trusted websites, but they are meant to exploit website users. A malicious script is injected into an otherwise trustworthy site through a vulnerability in the website's code. When a user accesses the infected website, they unknowingly run the bad code that would have access to cookies, session tokens, and other possibly sensitive and/or private information retained by the browser for that website.

SQL Injection

SQL injection is an attack hackers use to compromise a database server. With this type of attack, code is injected into a database through a vulnerability. This code may read or modify sensitive data inside the database. This attack probably would be used not directly against a user but rather against a business that has user data, much like XSS attacks.

Zero-Day

A zero-day vulnerability is a vulnerability discovered by attackers before the vendor has become aware of it, meaning no patch or fix exists to stop hackers. The term *zero-day* refers to the fact that a system or software company has only just learned of a vulnerability and effectively has zero days to fix it. Zero-day attacks aren't really a specific type of attack but rather an identification of when a system was vulnerable to a particular attack.

Combination Cyberattacks

It's important to note that malware often uses multiple types of attacks. For example, ransomware is often also a worm, copying itself to other vulnerable computers and infecting them with ransomware. Many phishing scams involve a virus. Cross-site scripting and SQL injection are often used to install Trojans and other viruses, making computers more susceptible to network penetration. Hackers frequently mix and match cyberattacks.

Why Do Hackers Hack?

Hackers hack for a variety of reasons. The most common reason is to gain access and exploit systems and information for monetary gain. This is why hacking often leads to identity theft and ransom demands.

Hacks can also be politically motivated. Many politically motivated hacks are meant to disrupt the target by shutting down or taking over their systems. Other hacks are done for bragging rights. It's not uncommon for hackers and hacking groups to announce that they are the ones who completed a hack in order to gain notoriety.

Still, other hacks are personal. Some people just want to make other people's lives miserable, often for revenge. Another personal reason is for education. Yes, hackers need practice too. And sometimes, they hack to educate organizations about the vulnerabilities in their systems.

As evidenced earlier in this section, not all hackers have the same motivations. In general, hackers fall into three different motivation categories:

1. **Black hat hackers:** When most people think of hackers, these are the types of hackers they are referring to. These are the bad hackers; they try to compromise systems mainly for monetary gain but also for ideological reasons. They use cyberattacks to hold computers hostage, access sensitive information, and destroy files.
2. **White hat hackers:** Sometimes referred to as "ethical hackers," white hat hackers are the antithesis of black hat hackers. They implement cyberattacks to find vulnerabilities that need fixing. They are often contracted by organizations to assess the security of a company's systems. Ethical hacking has grown in popularity over the years, and there are formal education pathways to it as a career.

3. **Gray hat hackers:** As you've probably guessed, these hackers lie somewhere in the middle of black and white hat hackers—the gray area if you will. Gray hats will often identify vulnerabilities that an organization has but will do so without the company's permission. Sometimes, they will simply notify the company so it can fix it. Sometimes, they may demand compensation for identifying the vulnerabilities and will exploit the vulnerability if they aren't paid. And sometimes, they'll put pressure on a company by telling them about the vulnerability and letting them know they will release the information about the vulnerability publicly at some date. This puts pressure on organizations to patch the vulnerabilities in a timely manner.

 ## How Do Cybercriminals Monetize Their Attacks?

Financial gain is one of the key motivations for hackers, but how do they make money from their cyberattacks? Hackers have an alarming number of ways to make money, which is a significant reason for the increasing rate of cyberattacks.

Cryptocurrency (e.g., Bitcoin, Ethereum, Litecoin) isn't evil in itself, but it has emboldened cybercriminals. Cryptocurrency allows cybercriminals to be paid anonymously because it is much harder to trace than other currency types. These days, almost all hackers extorting victims demand payment in a cryptocurrency.

Here are the most common ways cybercriminals monetize their attacks.

Ransoms

Ransomware is probably the most straightforward way for cybercriminals to profit off of their activities, and that's why it's a fast-growing type of attack. After encrypting files so organizations can't access them, ransomers demand money in order to decrypt the files. These days, a lot of individuals and companies decide that the easiest path is to pay the ransom, further emboldening these cybercriminals.

Selling Your Data

There is a large third-party market for illegally obtained sensitive data like usernames and passwords, credit card numbers, Social Security numbers, etc. Often the hackers who steal this information aren't the people that use them. There are buyers for all kinds of illegally obtained data who will use that data to commit identity theft and other fraud. These data sets are usually bought and sold on the dark web, which is part of the web accessible by only those with the proper anonymizing software.

Mining Cryptocurrencies

As detailed earlier, a bot is a machine a hacker has compromised and now controls. A network of these machines is called a botnet. Sometimes, cybercriminals use botnets to mine cryptocurrency. In short, cryptocurrency mining is a way of being rewarded by creating new coins of cryptocurrency. It takes a lot of computing power to mine cryptocurrency. Using compromised computers to do it is cost effective for crypto miners, because it adds bots to their computing power at no cost to them.

Selling Access

Sometimes, when hackers compromise computer networks and systems, they don't do anything harmful right away. If their hack has created a backdoor to a computer system that others may want, they may prefer to sell that access to someone else rather than use it themselves.

Extortion

Another reason a hacker may not do anything harmful right away is that they want to extort the victim. For example, they may have gotten access to sensitive financial records or intellectual property and may demand payment for not releasing the information. Gray hat hackers may also extort organizations by threatening to use and sell the ability to exploit a vulnerability they've found if that organization doesn't pay them.

Shorting Stocks

When an investor "shorts" a stock, they make money when the stock price falls. A hacker may short a stock and make money, knowing that they can anonymously cause significant enough harm to an organization to make their stock price fall.

Paid Job

While it is common for white hat hackers to be paid for their services, there are also paid black hat hackers for hire. There are firms that provide these services, and, of course, job listings on the dark web. Hackers can contract out their services and be paid based on performing a hack as opposed to profiting directly from the results of the hack.

In the Real World: Noteworthy Attacks of the Last 15 Years

So far, I've written about the different types of attacks cybercriminals can employ in theory. Over the last 15 years, there have been many high-profile cyberattacks. Here are a few of the more prominent and devastating attacks, with the type of attack in parentheses.

ZeuS Trojan (Trojan)

The attack: ZeuS, referred to as Zeus or Zbot, was first detected in 2007 when it was first used to steal information from the United States Department of Transportation and soon after to compromise the websites of companies like Bank of America, NASA, Monster.com, ABC, Oracle, and many more.

The exploit: ZeuS is a trojan horse malware package that runs on Microsoft Windows. It usually is deployed via phishing campaigns and malicious software downloads. Once a machine is infected, ZeuS steals information from web browsers (stored credentials, financial information, etc.) and variants can log keystrokes (i.e., keep track of everything typed through the keyboard). Any system infected with ZeuS also becomes a bot (hence, the alternative name Zbot). The hackers who deploy ZeuS can then use the infected systems to carry out other attacks.

The aftermath: This virus is still around today. Bits and pieces of the code are still in use in other viruses. ZeuS can be incredibly hard to detect because it can re-encrypt itself upon infecting a system.

Heartland Payment Systems (SQL Injection)

The attack: Heartland Payment Systems, which is a major payment processing provider, announced in January 2009 that its payment processing systems were breached by hackers. The hack actually occurred in 2008.

The exploit: Cybercriminals used SQL injection techniques to compromise a web form that allowed access to Heartland's corporate network. Once the hackers were able to access the corporate network, they worked to bypass other corporate security protocols and installed sniffer software that captured credit card data during payment transactions. Over 130 million credit/debit card accounts were compromised.

The aftermath: Within days of the announcement, Heartland stock dropped 50 percent, dropping 80 percent in early March 2009.

Operation Aurora (Zero-Day and Phishing)

The attack: In January 2010, Google announced that its corporate infrastructure had been breached by a highly sophisticated attack originating in China. Google detected the breach in December 2009. The attack also targeted at least 20 other large companies from various sectors (Internet, finance, media, and others).

The exploit: Operation Aurora was a sophisticated and coordinated series of attacks. It exploited zero-day vulnerabilities in Internet Explorer to compromise computers. Once the computers were compromised, a backdoor connection was created allowing hackers to control some functions of the computers. These compromised computers then searched for other vulnerable systems and stole intellectual property. The goal of the attacks was to gain access to, and potentially modify, source code repositories of high-tech security and defense contractors. The hackers were also performing counter-intelligence; they were trying to infiltrate the Gmail accounts of Chinese human rights activists and to uncover how much information the U.S. government had about Chinese spies operating in the United States.

Phishing was another key part of the Operation Aurora attacks. The hackers used highly targeted spear-phishing attacks to install malware that siphoned confidential information out of the targeted organizations.

The aftermath: Intellectual property was stolen from Google and other companies. Two Gmail accounts were compromised via the zero-day exploits. Due to the sensitive nature of the information involved, a lot of the specifics of what was compromised may never be made public.

Stuxnet (Worm)

The attack: The Stuxnet worm, which originally attacked Iran's nuclear facilities, was discovered in 2010.

The exploit: The worm was transmitted by means of USB sticks and spread through zero-day flaws in Microsoft Windows computers. It searched infected PCs for Siemens Step 7 software, which automates and monitors electro-mechanical equipment. The worm would then use the Internet to update its attack code and send damaging instructions to the electro-mechanical equipment. To keep itself from being detected, the worm sent false information back to the main controller to make it look like all systems were functioning properly.

The aftermath: Iranian equipment was destroyed, causing significant damage to Iran's nuclear program. Most cybersecurity experts believe that Stuxnet is a weapon developed by the United States and Israel; however, this statement remains hypothetical, with no official announcement made. Over time, other hackers have modified the code to target water treatment plants, power plants, and gas lines.

Sony PlayStation Network and Sony Online Entertainment (SQL Injection)

The attack: Sony reported that its home gaming PlayStation Network was breached in April 2011. The same hackers proceeded to break into Sony's multiplayer PC game service, Sony Online Entertainment, and music streaming service, Qriocity Video.

The exploit: The hackers used SQL injection to break into Sony's systems and stole credit card and/or personally identifiable information (login credentials, names, addresses, email addresses, phone numbers) from over 102 million users.

The aftermath: Sony had to take its PlayStation Network offline for more than three weeks. It offered subscribers 30 days of premium-level PlayStation Plus features in an effort to keep customers. In 2014, Sony Pictures Entertainment was also hacked, with as much as 100 TB of sensitive data being stolen. Unreleased movie content and embarrassing emails from executives were leaked online.

2012 U.S. Financial Institutions— Operation Ababil (DDoS)

The attack: In September 2012, Bank of America, JPMorgan Chase, Wells Fargo, Citigroup, and several other U.S. financial institutions suffered outages due to a coordinated cyberattack from Iranian hackers.

The exploit: The hackers initially compromised various web servers around the world with unpatched vulnerabilities and turned them into bots. They then used those bots to direct more than 60 Gbps worth of data at U.S. financial institution web and application servers, overwhelming them and shutting them down. The attacks targeted different financial institutions throughout the year.

The aftermath: DDoS attacks are meant to inflict damage, not to expose private data. These were politically motivated attacks that cost these banks and customers untold millions and harmed their reputations. In 2016, the U.S. indicted seven Iranian residents for the crimes.

Target (Phishing)

The attack: In December 2013, big-box retailer Target announced that its point-of-sale systems had been breached. The systems had actually been breached in November, right around Black Friday.

The exploit: Attackers sent phishing emails to Target vendors, which allowed them to hijack their access to Target's corporate networks. The emails contained Trojans that intercepted the vendor's login credentials. Cybercriminals used the credentials to hack their way to Target's point-of-sale systems, where they installed malware that allowed them to grab credit/debit card information every time a card was swiped. Over 110 million credit/debit card accounts including personally identifiable information and credit/debit card numbers were compromised.

The aftermath: Target eventually settled a class-action lawsuit originating from this hack and agreed to pay up to $10,000 to affected customers.

Ashley Madison (unknown)

The attack: In July 2015, a hacker group calling itself "The Impact Team" stole user data from Ashley Madison, a commercial website specializing in enabling extramarital affairs. Identifying data of users who were members of the site was posted publicly.

The exploit: No one is sure how exactly Ashley Madison was compromised. The hackers threatened to release sensitive emails sent by executives and private user information (names, email addresses, physical addresses, usernames, passwords, and phone numbers) if the owners of the site didn't shut it down. The cybercriminals released data in multiple data dumps, exposing sensitive information from the company and users. Ironically, a couple of months before the hack was announced, Ashley Madison's director of security warned executives via emails about multiple cross-site scripting vulnerabilities in their codebase. The hackers released these emails as part of the hack.

The aftermath: Ashley Madison ended up paying $11.2 million to settle dozens of data breach lawsuits. Many websites popped up (and still exist) that allow anyone to easily browse and search the leaked data. More than 11 million accounts were leaked. Bad actors used this information in attempts to extort many people.

Mirai (Botnet)

The attack: In September 2016, the Mirai botnet temporarily crippled several critical Internet infrastructure services that made much of the Internet inaccessible on the U.S. East Coast.

The exploit: A Rutgers University undergraduate named Paras Jha led a hacking group whose original intention was to cripple Minecraft servers so they could make more money as customers moved to *their* Minecraft servers. Mirai targeted vulnerable Internet of Things (IoT) devices (i.e., smart devices that connect to the Internet) such as routers and network cameras, using a variety of techniques, including exploiting devices still using default passwords. Once the device was compromised, Mirai would destroy any existing malware on the device and give full command of the device to Jha and his team. Each device would also scan local networks for other devices to infect. Then, all those bots were used to perform DDoS attacks on important Internet infrastructure service providers, causing them to go down and making the Internet inaccessible for many people for hours.

The aftermath: In December 2016, Jha and his associates pled guilty to crimes perpetrated by the Mirai attacks. Unfortunately, the code used in Mirai is publicly available, and many hackers have modified and deployed it in their own attacks over the years.

WannaCry (Ransomware)

The attack: In May 2017, WannaCry was unleashed in Asia and eventually spread across the world. It encrypted the files of the computers it infected and then demanded a ransom in cryptocurrency in order for users and companies to access their files again.

The exploit: Cybersecurity experts believe the malware was initially transmitted through open Server Message Block (SMB) ports, which are ports used for sharing files between computers. WannaCry primarily infected Windows 7 computers. After encrypting files, it traveled through computer networks as a worm, copying itself to other vulnerable computers, encrypting their files, and then demanding a ransom to decrypt the files. Within a day, it infected more than 230,000 computers in over 150 countries.

The attackers initially demanded BTC 300. Later, they increased that amount to BTC 600 and threatened that the victims' files would be permanently deleted if they didn't pay the ransom within three days. Most, if not all, people who paid never got their files back.

The aftermath: One of the largest agencies compromised by WannaCry was the National Health Service (NHS), which operates hospitals and other medical services in most parts of the UK. Reportedly, computers, MRI scanners, and blood-storage refrigerators in England and Scotland were all affected. NHS had to suspend some non-critical emergency services and reroute ambulances while trying to recover from the hack. A patch that would have prevented WannaCry from infecting a computer had already been released by Microsoft a few weeks earlier, but many individuals and organizations don't apply patches in a timely manner. It's estimated that WannaCry caused US$4 billion in losses across the globe.

Equifax (Network Penetration)

The attack: In September 2017, credit bureau Equifax announced that its systems had been breached. Data that was stolen included names, addresses, dates of birth, Social Security numbers, driver's license numbers, and credit card numbers. The breach was thought to have begun in May 2017.

The exploit: A vulnerability was discovered in the Apache Struts software that Equifax used for systems handling credit disputes from customers. Equifax neglected to apply a key security patch for it that was released on March 7, 2017. Hackers took advantage of this security hole to gain access to internal servers on Equifax's corporate network. They then searched credit-monitoring databases and used encryption to mask their activities while extracting information in small temporary archives so Equifax wouldn't notice.

The aftermath: Over 160 million private records were compromised in the breach, making it one of the largest identity theft cybercrimes ever. Equifax stock dropped 13 percent the day after the breach was made public. Hundreds of consumers and the Federal Trade

Commission (FTC) successfully sued Equifax for over US$500 million in damages.

Facebook Data Breaches and Leaks (Multiple Attacks)

The attack: Facebook had a series of data breaches and leaks that affected over a billion accounts between 2018 and 2021. Some of the attacks exploited vulnerabilities in Facebook's infrastructure. Other leaks occurred when user data was accidentally shared with third-party developers and Facebook employees.

The exploit: Let's review some of the data breaches and leaks:

- In March 2018, Facebook exposed the data of 87 million users to the political consulting firm Cambridge Analytica. Cambridge Analytica exploited a loophole in Facebook's API, which enabled it to grab data from the Facebook friends of people who had given Cambridge Analytica consent. The data included personal information about where users lived and what pages they liked.
- In September 2018, hackers exploited Facebook's "View as" feature, which allows users to view their profile as if they were another user, by stealing access tokens that gave them the ability to view profile information meant to be private. The hackers accessed up to 90 million user profiles.
- In March 2019, a report found that as many as 600 million Facebook user passwords were available in

plaintext on an internal Facebook server. The server wasn't publicly available, but at least 2,000 Facebook employees had access to them.

- In April 2019, researchers found 540 million Facebook records stored on a public server. These records contained Facebook IDs, account names, comments, reactions, likes, and more. This turned out to be the mistake of app developers who improperly stored the data.

- In June 2020, Facebook developers discovered that third-party developers had access to personal user data, which they should not have had, similar to Cambridge Analytica in 2018. Thousands of developers could have accessed data they weren't supposed to.

The aftermath: For years, Cambridge Analytica sold the data they exploited. There are multiple instances of troves of Facebook user data being posted publicly on servers throughout this timeline. Likely, the data came from one of these breaches or leaks.

Colonial Pipeline (Ransomware)

The attack: In May 2021, the oil supplier Colonial Pipeline suffered an attack that for six days crippled its ability to manage its gas, jet fuel, and oil pipelines that served Houston, TX, and many other southeastern states in the U.S.

The exploit: The hackers, identified by the FBI as the criminal hacking group named DarkSide, targeted Colonial Pipeline's billing infrastructure through a virtual private network (VPN) account that was no longer in use. This account, however, still had remote access to the company's computer network because it hadn't been deactivated. The password to this account was found on the dark web, indicating that the Colonial Pipeline employee that used it may have used the same password on another account that had been previously hacked. No one knows for certain how the password was obtained.

The hackers used this account to install ransomware on the company's billing machines. Although Colonial Pipeline could still control the flow of their pipelines, it shut them all down, because it could not accurately bill for consumption and was concerned that other systems that could actually cause damage to the pipeline were compromised.

The hackers also stole 100 GB of data, which they also threatened to leak if the ransom wasn't paid.

The aftermath: This was the largest cyberattack on oil infrastructure in U.S. history. The Federal Motor Carrier Safety Administration issued an emergency declaration for 17 states and Washington, DC, to keep fuel supply lines open by allowing more petroleum products to be transported by road and rail than is normally permitted. Despite the emergency declarations, American Airlines had to change flight schedules temporarily to adjust to the reduced fuel availability for some flights. Gas prices in many southeastern states hit five-year highs.

Colonial Pipeline paid the hackers BTC 75 (worth US$4.4 million at the time). The hackers then provided the company with the tools to get the systems up and running again. The Department of Justice eventually recovered BTC 63.7 (worth approximately US$2.3 million).

What I Do: Monitoring Exploits and Breaches in Case They Affect Me

The list of breaches listed in the previous section is just a small sample of the total number of breaches that took place over the last few years. Although most newsworthy hacks and breaches deal with companies, some (e.g., Mirai) directly target regular consumers.

Keeping track of breaches lets me know when I may need to take some specific actions to protect myself from being hacked or to protect my identity if an organization that has my data has been hacked. What do I do to protect myself? That's the subject of Part 2 of this book.

Key Takeaways

☐ The term *cybersecurity* refers to the measures taken to protect computer networks, devices, and data from unauthorized or criminal use. It is also the practice of ensuring confidentiality, integrity, and availability of information.

- ☐ This book focuses on *personal cybersecurity*, which spotlights the practices individuals and families should take to protect themselves from cybercriminals.
- ☐ Cybersecurity dates back to the 1970s.
- ☐ A program named Creeper, written in 1971, is widely considered as the first computer virus.
- ☐ Cybercriminals have regularly been using malware to steal information, take control of computers, and shut down computer systems since the 1980s.
- ☐ Cybersecurity is important for the following reasons:
  - ☐ More and more of our everyday lives and activities require us to use systems susceptible to cybercriminals.
  - ☐ The number of cyberattacks is increasing.
  - ☐ The time and monetary costs of recovering from a cyberattack can be substantial.
- ☐ Cyberattacks are on the rise for the following reasons:
  - ☐ There are more online services and more people using them.
  - ☐ More people are working remotely.
  - ☐ Cryptocurrency makes monetizing cyberattacks easier.
  - ☐ Companies and individuals frequently pay the ransoms demanded by cybercriminals.
  - ☐ Cyberattacks are a safer way to attack a country or part of a country for politically motivated hackers.
  - ☐ Ransomware-as-a-service has significantly lowered the technological barrier to entry for ransomware crimes.
- ☐ The main types of cyberattacks are as follows:
  - ☐ Viruses
  - ☐ Worms

- ☐ Trojans
- ☐ Spyware
- ☐ Ransomware
- ☐ Brute-force attacks
- ☐ Phishing
- ☐ Social engineering
- ☐ Denial-of-service/Distributed   denial-of-service (DoS/DDoS)
- ☐ DNS spoofing
- ☐ Man-in-the-middle (MitM)
- ☐ Cross-site scripting (XSS)
- ☐ SQL injection
- ☐ Zero-day
- ☐ Real-world cyberattacks are most often a combination of different types of attacks.
- ☐ The reasons hackers hack include the following:
  - ☐ Monetary gain
  - ☐ Political reasons
  - ☐ Notoriety
  - ☐ Educating organizations about their vulnerabilities
  - ☐ Personal reasons (revenge, education)
- ☐ The three basic types of hackers are as follows:
  - ☐ Black hat hackers
  - ☐ White hat hackers
  - ☐ Gray hat hackers
- ☐ Cybercriminals monetize their attacks by doing the following:
  - ☐ Demanding ransoms
  - ☐ Selling your data
  - ☐ Mining cryptocurrency
  - ☐ Selling access to systems

- ☐ Extortion
- ☐ Shorting stocks
- ☐ There have been many high-profile cyberattacks in the last 15 years.

Part 2

Best Practices for Safeguarding Your Privacy and Protecting Yourself from Cyberattacks and Data Breaches

Can Protecting Yourself Really Make a Difference?

After getting acquainted with all the noteworthy hacks and breaches of the last few years, you may have noticed that most of them involve large organizations. Cybercriminals often put more effort into attacking large organizations due to the impact and the potentially large payouts. If large companies with your data are being hacked, and you have little control over those companies exposing your data, how can you protect yourself?

There are a couple of answers to that question. First, hackers do target individuals and families, but this fact just doesn't make the news as often. You still need to protect your sensitive data, accounts, electronic devices, and home network from being hacked. Second, there are practices you can take on that can limit the amount of your private data a company exposes in a breach and the consequences of such exposure. In this part of the book, I'll go through the best practices for protecting yourself from cybercriminals of all kinds.

An illustration of some of the cybersecurity practices that can protect your family

Use Unique Strong Passwords for Everything

First and foremost, you should never reuse passwords. Hackers will often use a password that was found as part of a breach in one system to break into that user's accounts on other platforms. If one system you use is breached and you reuse passwords, there's a much higher chance that a hacker will access your other accounts. In fact, that's probably how Colonial Pipeline was compromised.

The best way to use unique passwords for all your accounts is to use a password manager like LastPass or Dashlane to manage all your passwords. Password managers can be used on computers and mobile devices to generate a unique password for every account. All you have to remember is the master password for the password manager. They can be configured to generate and input passwords when you visit websites or log in to apps.

The average American Internet user has 150 online accounts that require a password.[3] If you don't use a password manager and you don't repeat passwords, you'd have to remember 150 different passwords! If you choose not to use a password manager, a good password that you come up with on your own is a hard-to-guess but easy-for-you-to-remember phrase or sentence that is at least 15 characters long.

Know When to Change Your Passwords

Conventional wisdom says you should change your passwords every few months. But conventional wisdom is changing. Most cybersecurity experts (including me) don't recommend changing your password unless it is (1) weak (short and/or easy to guess), (2) used with other accounts, or (3) possibly compromised.

Part of the reason for this conventional wisdom change is people's tendency to replace their passwords with weaker ones. This is another area where password managers can help. Change your passwords as often as you like using

---

[3]   Michelle Caruthers, "World Password Day: How to Improve Your Passwords," *Dashlane* (blog), accessed August 23, 2022, https://blog. dashlane.com/world-password-day/.

a password manager as long as you always pick strong passwords.

How do you know when your password may be compromised? Here are a few ways:

1. Pay attention to popular cybersecurity news. Mainstream media usually reports on large companies suffering data breaches. If it is a company that you keep an account with, investigate to see whether you need to change your password.
2. Pay attention to unusual activity in your accounts. Many accounts will flag and notify you of suspicious login behavior. Google, Facebook, Twitter, and many more do this.
3. Register at Have I Been Pwned[4] to be notified if your email or phone number is part of a public data leak.
4. Many password managers have a feature that will prompt you to change your password if your credentials are found as part of a public data leak. Make sure to follow the advice of the password manager.

Even if you just suspect that your account may be compromised, you should consider changing your password to another one that is strong and unique. Also, if a device, such as a tablet, mobile phone, computer, or laptop is stolen or compromised, you should change the passwords to all accounts that you accessed with that device.

---

4   https://haveibeenpwned.com/.

Use Multi-factor Authentication

While having strong and unique passwords greatly helps your personal cybersecurity, they'll still fail to protect you if somehow they are leaked or hacked. However, using multi-factor authentication can thwart hackers from accessing your accounts, even if they have your passwords. Everyone should use some form of multi-factor authentication if it is available to them.

What is multi-factor authentication? Multi-factor authentication describes security technologies and practices that require multiple methods of authentication in order to access a system. These authentication methods include the following:

- **Something you know** – password, passphrase, or personal identification number (PIN)
- **Something you have** – token, smartcard, or key
- **Something you are** – biometrics like a fingerprint, voice recognition, or a retinal scan

You've probably been using multi-factor authentication for years. When you go to an ATM machine to withdraw money, you insert an ATM card (something you have) and then enter a PIN (something you know). This is using multiple methods, or factors, to authenticate that you are you and can have access to your bank account.

Multi-factor authentication can use 2, 3, 4, or more methods of authentication. Two-factor authentication, or 2FA, is a type of multi-factor authentication that requires only two methods. The ATM example above is 2FA. Your bank emailing or texting you a one-time authorization code when you log in to their website is also 2FA.

Most people already use some form of 2FA. There's the ATM card/PIN example I mentioned before. And most people are familiar with services that send you a code via email or text. Some even use 2FA authenticator apps on mobile phones like Google Authenticator and Duo. All these methods are better than just having a password, but they aren't all equivalent. Let's walk through the popular 2FA methods and briefly discuss their security.

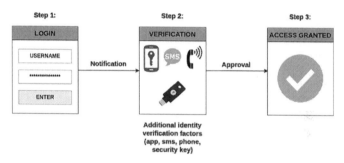

Figure 3. An illustration of the way multi-factor authentication works.

OK 2FA Methods

Email, text, and voice-call codes are the most common 2FA methods, but they are the least safe. They usually consist of a temporary four-to-eight-character code sent via email, text/SMS, or via a voice call to your phone. The service you are trying to log in to automatically generates the code. You enter the code when asked after logging in with your username and password. The code is usually good for a few minutes. One advantage of using voice-call codes is that they can work with landlines.

There are a few problems with this method. Emails, texts and phone calls are usually unencrypted. Texts and voice calls are also tied to a specific phone number that can be spoofed more easily than something tied to a specific device. Someone who has stolen your phone number or possibly changed your account to forward calls or texts to a second number, or who works at a cellular carrier, can easily intercept this code.

It's unfortunate that this is the most common 2FA method and often the only choice providers give you. It is way better than not having any 2FA, but there are better methods.

Good 2FA Methods

Push codes sent to an app on your phone are a step up from those sent via text or voice calls. They are encrypted and can be sent to only those devices where you've set up the authenticator app. Later iPhones have this ability built into the OS.

Authenticator apps can generate codes instead of having codes pushed to them or the phone. The service you use has to support the app. The service and app set up a secret private key (a derived or randomly generated string of characters) and then share a time-based algorithm that uses the secret key to generate valid codes. They have the advantage of not needing a cellular connection or even a Wi-Fi connection to work. Duo Mobile, LastPass Authenticator, Microsoft Authenticator, and Authy are popular apps that have this functionality.

Code-generating hardware tokens (usually small cards or keychain devices) used to be popular in many large corporations. They work in pretty much the same way as code-generating authenticator apps. However, smartphone authenticator apps, which are more convenient and less expensive to set up and maintain, have been taking over.

While these methods are pretty safe, they all still use temporary codes, which are susceptible to phishing attacks. Criminals can create fake duplicate sites meant to trick you into thinking you are logging in to the real site. Then you enter a code from your authenticator app, and the criminal takes the credentials you entered and the code and enters them into the real site to gain access to your account. This has happened even with Google accounts!

Better 2FA Methods

A step up from codes, push approvals don't require any type of code to be synchronized or generated. You use a service or an authenticator app to just select "Yes" or "Approve" when prompted for a second authentication, which comes from the service you're trying to log in to. Services like Microsoft, Google, and Yahoo have this capability. My employer uses Duo Mobile to do this. Authenticator apps like Duo Mobile can handle push approvals from multiple services.

One small problem with this method is that malicious mobile apps can fake or hijack push notifications to get someone to mistakenly authorize an account login. Still, this is significantly less risky than the previous methods discussed.

The Best 2FA Method

The best 2FA method widely available to consumers is physical security keys, like USB security keys. USB security keys are small devices that plug into your computer's USB port. Some USB security keys also support near-field communication (NFC) and/or Bluetooth and thus can interact with smartphones, tablets, and laptops without being plugged into them.

USB security keys are sometimes called U2F (Universal 2nd Factor) keys. They have a small chip with all the security protocols and a code that allow them to connect with services to verify your identity. The keys work with popular web browsers like Google Chrome to connect to identity verification services.

First, you register the key with the service(s) where you want to enable 2FA. When you log in to the service, you'll be prompted for 2FA verification from your key. Then you simply plug your key into your computer's USB slot and tap it to verify your identity.

What makes hardware keys better than the other options? There's no security code used, so standard phishing attacks won't work. There's not necessarily an app involved in using the key, so malicious apps won't work either. A hacker will need access to the physical key to break into your account.

The downside of security keys is that they aren't free. They aren't expensive, but apps and text messages are basically free.

You won't always be able to pick and choose a type of multi-factor authentication. Many service providers support only some of them, and some don't support any at all. However, whenever you can, use some form of multi-factor authentication.

 # Social Media Cybersecurity Best Practices

Social media can be great for sharing information, consuming information, and connecting with people, but it also is a treasure trove of opportunities for cybercriminals to exploit. Here are some of the cybersecurity issues with social media and the ways you can protect yourself.

Protecting Your Identity and Privacy on Social Media

You may have published a lot of information about yourself on social media, which can help cybercriminals commit identity theft and fraud. Have you looked at how much information you share in your profiles? Or the personal details you share in posts and tweets? In general, to protect yourself from cyberattacks you should refrain from sharing the following:

- Your location data (GPS coordinates, IP address, etc.). Make sure the social media service you are using removes location data from pictures that you upload, or remove the location data yourself.
- Self-identifying information (e.g., your full name with your middle name; your date of birth; photos of passports, credit cards, and driver's licenses). This includes information you may use as the answers to security questions like the name of your first pet, the place you were born, your mother's maiden name, etc.
- Pictures of the exterior of a new home you just bought. Cybercriminals will use this information in phishing attacks and in trying to commit identity fraud.
- Photos of your young children and grandchildren. Photos, combined with names and other information, can be used to commit identity theft. The problem with identity theft of young children's information is that no one usually checks their credit record. When those children become adults, they may find they already have a 10-year bad credit and banking history that they have to fix.

Now, I know some of this seems drastic. If you are tightly controlling whom you share information with, you can share some of these things on social media (like pictures of your children). But if you don't fully trust or know everyone you are sharing this information with, then you shouldn't be doing it, which leads me to my next recommendation.

Don't "Friend" or "Connect" on Social Media with People Whom You Don't Know

Although this advice is most applicable to Facebook and LinkedIn, it more generally applies to other social media networks like Instagram (e.g., whom you allow to follow you). Your Facebook and LinkedIn profiles are a goldmine for identity thieves. One way these fraudsters try to compromise your identity is by getting access to more details about you by becoming part of your social media network. The types of things that are on your profiles include the following:

- Where you live
- Where you work
- Whom you are related to
- Where you went to school
- Your contact information

This information in the wrong hands can lead to a lot of fraud. It also gives a scammer more ways to contact you and attack you with phishing scams (like private messages via Facebook Messenger).

On Facebook especially, accepting a friend request also gives that person more information about your friends. For example, a stranger that you accept as a friend can see photos that you and your friends are tagged in and posts that your friends make on your timeline.

Beware of Fake Profiles (Impersonation)

Another way scammers attack after friending you is by cloning your account. Once they are your friend, they can use that information to create a profile looking just like yours and then use that account to communicate with people you know, posing as you, in order to get access to those people's information and run scams on them, which becomes much easier because those people think they are interacting with you.

You could also be the target of someone impersonating someone you know on social media. Make sure you really know whom you converse and share information with. A message may come from an account looking like your friend's, but that doesn't mean the account is your friend's. Here are a few tips about how to spot a fake profile. None of these are foolproof, and they don't all necessarily mean the profile you are dealing with is fake. However, you should become skeptical if you notice the following:

- They use the default avatar instead of a personal picture.
- Their profile picture looks like it could be a stock photo. How do you know whether it is a stock photo or a photo taken from another site? Upload the image to Google Images[5] and do a search.

---

[5] https://www.google.com/imghp.

- The name of the account doesn't match what you think it should be. Maybe it has a lot of numbers because the real account name is taken. Maybe the username doesn't match the name at all.
- A bio is incomplete or blank. The bio may be incomplete or blank because the scammer doesn't know enough information.
- The account doesn't have any posts. If the account hasn't posted any content, pictures, etc., it may just be a shell account impersonating someone's profile.

Again, a real friend's account may have some of these attributes. However, if an account has a few of these, you should definitely take some time to be sure the account is legitimate.

Be Careful with Your Social Media Privacy Settings

Unless you are an influencer or some other type of public figure, you don't want to have your information available for anyone to see on Facebook and Instagram. Even public figures and influencers have (1) private accounts that they want to protect and (2) public accounts. At a minimum, you probably want to limit who can see your profile, photos, and posts on both platforms. Privacy on social media isn't just about stopping cybercriminals from targeting you. Sometimes, you don't want advertisers or other people to target you. Or you may just want to keep more of your information private from Facebook and other companies. Let's go through the privacy settings I recommend for Facebook and for Instagram. Note that in the Appendix you'll find instructions for configuring these settings.

For Facebook

- Restrict who can see your personal posts. You probably want your posts visible to your friends. If so, make sure your posts don't default to being public. Keep in mind that when you post or comment in a public group, your post or comment will be public regardless of your personal settings. Also, when you post on another person's profile, that person controls who sees your post.
- Disable third-party apps from accessing your Facebook data. This is how the Cambridge Analytica scandal referenced in an earlier section occurred. Facebook has since allowed its users to control whether third-party apps can harvest their data.
- Restrict Facebook from tracking Off-Facebook Activity. This stops companies from sending the information they track about you (i.e., what you do on their site) back to Facebook. This isn't necessarily a way for cybercriminals to get at you. However, if you are concerned about privacy, this setting may be of interest to you. Keep in mind that this also stops you from using your Facebook login to log in to sites which is good for protecting the privacy of your data.
- Hide your location. Facebook uses location data to choose what news and products to send to you. Again, this isn't necessarily a way for cybercriminals to attack you, but it's important if you care about this part of your privacy.

- Stop Google from showing your Facebook account. By default, Google indexes your Facebook profile page. That means that anyone using Google to search for your name will be able to find your profile page and any publicly visible data on it.
- Stop Facebook from advertising your activity. By default, Facebook automatically uses your ad likes to target those ads to your friends. Your friends may see that you liked that ad. You can set your interests to be private so this doesn't happen.

In addition to these settings, I recommend that you occasionally clean up your friends list. Make sure that everyone on it is a person you want to share your profile and posts with. Also, make sure everyone on there is who they say they are.

For Instagram

Instagram has fewer privacy settings than Facebook. Also, you can't keep parent company Meta (owner of Facebook and Instagram) from sending your Instagram data to Facebook. However, there are still some Instagram privacy settings you should consider:

- Make your posts inaccessible to strangers. By default, Instagram makes your account and posts visible to anyone using the app. You can change this to make sure other users have to send you a follow request that you accept before they can see your posts. Note that changing this won't affect the ability of those who already follow you to see your posts.

- Stop Instagram from tracking your location. Instagram uses location to allow you to automatically tag your posts with location information. However, Instagram also uses that information to pick which ads to send you and to recommend content from people you don't follow. You may be okay with that. But you should also know that this data is used by Facebook and other companies that Meta does advertising business with to track and target you with ads as well.

- Limit the ways Instagram Stories can be shared. By default, anyone who has access to your Instagram Stories can repost them on their account and share them with friends. You can limit the ways your Stories can be shared by (1) allowing them to be seen by only a "close friends list" that you create and/or (2) disabling sharing of your Stories.

- Limit how much data is shared with third-party apps and services, since this type of sharing led to the Cambridge Analytica scandal. Instagram lets you control what data is shared with third parties other than Facebook.

- Don't share/sync your contacts with Instagram. Instagram uses your contacts to suggest accounts for you to follow. If you never take away the permission to access your contact list, Instagram will periodically scan your contacts. Instagram and Facebook may also use this information to target ads to your friends.

- Limit the ways Instagram can recommend your account to others. Many people on Instagram want as many followers as possible. Others would rather pick and choose exactly who is in their network. If you fall more towards the latter category, you should change the setting that allows your account to be recommended to others when Instagram proposes "similar accounts" to users.

Beware of Social Media Phishing and Malware Attacks

Social media sites are popular platforms for phishing and malware attacks. Links in posts can take you to sites that contain malware or try to get your information to use later in fraud. Beware of clicking on links to sites that make promises too good to be true or that look sketchy. Also beware of clicking on links that obscure the true domain of the site by using a link shortener (e.g., bit.ly, ow.ly, and tinyurl.com). There are perfectly legitimate uses for link shorteners, and I use them as well; however sometimes, they are simply meant to hide the true destination of a link.

Protect Yourself from Data Harvesting

Playing games, participating in surveys and personality quizzes, and answering viral sets of questions about oneself are favorite pastimes of social media users. Although such activities can be fun, they can also be really dangerous. Have you ever thought about what these surveys and quizzes do with the information you give them? Do you ever answer any questions with information that could be used to answer security questions or otherwise compromise your identity? Many of these activities on social media are light-hearted fun, but others look to monetize, or worse, exploit your data by scamming you or people who know you by impersonating you. I recommend limiting what types of information you provide about yourself in games, surveys, personality quizzes, and general posts on social media.

Watch Out for Malicious Third-Party Apps

Third-party apps may access some of your social media account information. Popular reasons to do this are to play games or to log in to accounts, using your social media login. The problem is that third-party apps can copy and store data from your social media account on their servers. They can then use this data in ways you didn't intend, such as sharing it with other parties. It also means your data is now stored in another place that could be breached.

You should review which apps you've given third-party access to across Facebook and other platforms. Make sure you understand the ways these apps are going to use your data. Be sure that letting them have your data is worth it. Also, be sure you know what data you share with them. Remove access to any apps you don't use, don't need to have integrated with your social media account, or don't trust.

Protecting Yourself on Social Media Is about More than Cybercrimes

Be careful when talking about the things you've bought and the vacations you're about to take. Although this information isn't necessarily a threat for cyberattacks, it can make your home a target for would-be thieves. Consider limiting how much you share about vacations until after you've returned, or at least be sure you share that information with people you trust only, which on many social media platforms is hard to be sure of.

Limit How Much You Are Tracked on the Internet

Someone is always trying to track you when you are on the Internet. Some of the ways we are tracked include the following:

- IP addresses – Your Internet Protocol (IP) address is effectively your device's address on the Internet. It's how the services you use know how to send your device their content (e.g., emails, chat messages, audio and video streams, etc.). IP addresses can also be used to help companies track you across different devices and even figure out your physical location.

- Location services – In the section on best practices, we looked at stopping sites and apps from tracking your location multiple times, because your location is often used to track you on the Internet. While there are times when an app absolutely has to have your device location to provide its service (like when Netflix needs to verify your region to find out which content it can serve you, or when Google Maps needs to give you directions), there are many instances when you may not want an app to track your location.

- Tracking IDs – Websites use IDs in "cookies" (data files stored in your browser) to keep track of who you are and what activities you partake in when you visit. They enable advertising networks like the ones run by Google and Facebook to keep track of your activity as you visit different websites. Computers and mobile devices are tracked this way.

- Signing into accounts – Have you ever wondered why all your favorite sites want you to create an account, even if they aren't going to charge you for most, or all, of their content and services? It's so that they can track you more accurately. Google always prompts you to login or create an account. Facebook won't even work without an account. Some of these services partner with ad networks to connect your activity across accounts.

You may be okay with some of these ways and reasons you are tracked. But if you don't feel comfortable being tracked, here are ways to limit the number of companies following you around the Internet:

- Turning on the "Do not track" request in your browser – Most browsers have a setting where you can tell websites not to track you. Not all sites will honor this request, but many will.
- Not allowing sites to save cookies – Most reputable sites ask you for permission to use cookies when you first visit them. Simply click "no" when asked. This may disable some features of the website, but that's the price you pay to cut down on trackers.
- Using Internet-tracking blockers – There are several browser plug-ins that can help protect you from

Internet tracking. Some plug-ins can also block the ads you would normally see on many sites.

- Using search engines that won't track you – Google is the de facto standard in search engines, but Google logs what you search for and uses trackers to serve you ads. Google also uses this information and other information it has stored about you to tailor your search results. Search engines like DuckDuckGo, Mojeek, and StartPage track and store significantly less information about you, and they anonymize what they store.

- Disabling location services on your phone – You can disable your location services completely on your phone, or you can go app by app and restrict apps from accessing your location. Note that some apps may not work properly, or at all, without location services.

- Using a VPN when connecting to the Internet – Whether you are home or on public Wi-Fi, your devices always broadcast their IP address to whatever services you connect to. If you connect to the Internet, using a VPN, the address that the services you connect to see is the one your VPN provided you with. A VPN can also obscure what services you use on the Internet in case you want to keep those private.

In this section, we have looked at ways of limiting how much you are tracked on the Internet. These steps eliminate most tracking. However, even if you implement them all, there are still ways to track you.

How to Protect Yourself from Phishing and Other Social Engineering Attacks

Recall that social engineering attacks are when a cyber-criminal tricks someone into revealing personal information (e.g., Social Security number, banking and credit card information, etc.) or doing something they wouldn't normally do. Social engineering attacks can be low tech (e.g., phone call surveys, acting like a friend in public, posing as someone in authority, etc.) or high tech (e.g., faked websites, emails with malicious links, etc.). Many ransomware and other high-profile cyberattacks occurred in large part due to phishing or other forms of social engineering. Here are some tips to protect yourself from these types of attacks:

- Always be suspicious of unsolicited phone calls, visits, and emails from individuals asking about sensitive information. If at all possible, verify that the person and/or organization they represent is legitimate and has a valid reason for contacting you and asking for information.

- When someone asks you for private information, always make sure it is absolutely needed. You should always be skeptical before you decide to give out sensitive personal information. Be sure you know why they need your information. If the reason is unclear, don't give it out. I can't tell you how many times I've been asked for a Social Security number via in-person forms and online. I've found that asking what the person needs this information for (or whether they need it at all) has cut down on the number of times I've had to give it out. It turns out that even legitimate organizations often ask for information they don't need (which gives them more information to divulge if they are hacked).

- Don't provide personal or financial information in an email. Even when dealing with institutions that you may think need your information for a legitimate purpose, always ask for a secure portal to transfer information. A phishing cybercriminal probably doesn't have an official-looking secure portal set up if they contact you via email. Also, emails aren't secure.

- Don't give a website sensitive information without verifying the site's identity and security. Pay attention to the URL of a site. If you are at all unsure about the URL, you should Google the domain to see whether it is legitimate before uploading any information. A common ploy is for malicious websites to use a very similar-sounding domain with a slightly different spelling or a .net domain instead of a .com (note that most .net addresses are legitimate domains). Also, make sure the site uses a valid HTTPS certificate so that your information is sent over the Internet encrypted.

- Make sure the link you click on takes you to the site you think it is. A common ploy for phishing emails is to list completely legitimate website addresses in an email. However, the link connected to the listed address actually takes you to a different site. Sometimes, this site will look exactly like the legitimate site, with the aim of getting you to enter your information. Always, always, always double-check the URL of the site you visit to make sure it is legit. One method many people employ is to never click on links in emails. They cut and paste or retype links to avoid the described problem. If the email uses a link shortener, you can check where the link really goes to by using a service like getlinkinfo.com.

- Take advantage of anti-phishing features offered by your email clients and web browsers. For example, Gmail cautions you about certain emails if it thinks they may be malicious. It also scans attachments for viruses. Google Chrome usually blocks or warns you when going to sites where it can't verify the SSL certificate, the certificate has expired, or it has been reported as malicious. You can ignore these warnings at your own risk, but please pay attention to them.

- Verify email addresses to make sure messages really come from where they say they come. Spoofing email addresses (faking them) is common because it is easy to do. But email servers have ways of verifying email addresses via Sender Policy Framework (SPF) records, DomainKeys Identified Mail (DKIM) authentication, and Domain-based Message Authentication, Reporting & Conformance (DMARC) authentication. These are all types of standard information that email servers receive with an email. Your email provider probably uses these fields to flag emails as spam, but they still miss flagging some malicious emails, so look at unexpected emails with a skeptical eye. If you determine that an email isn't legitimate (more on how I do that later in this section), be sure to report it to your email service provider. This helps them auto-matically filter out similar emails in future.

- Don't post too much personal information about yourself on social media. I mentioned this in the section on social media, but it is worth repeating. Cybercriminals use this information to help bolster their credibility with you and/or someone you know, making their social engineering attacks much more effective.

What I Do: Checking whether Emails Come from a Legitimate Sender

In the previous section, I mentioned that many email providers often use SPF records, DKIM, and DMARC authentication to determine whether an email is spam or malicious. The problem is that you have little control over how they interpret this information. Sometimes, mali-cious emails that fail or don't fully pass one of these checks still get through. If I am suspicious of an email, I often scrutinize it. Here is what I look for:

- Sender's address matching the company – Legitimate organizations usually send messages from email addresses that contain the company's domain name (e.g., an email from an Apple employee would probably be something like name@apple.com). If it is an email claiming to be from a well-known company, then it should probably come from the company's domain, not a name email provider like Gmail, Yahoo, MSN, etc. Sometimes, spammers use deceptive domains (e.g., applesupport.com or apple1.com instead of apple.com). Watch out for these.

- Spelling and other grammatical errors – If an email from an organization, especially a well-known organization, contains multiple spelling or other grammatical errors, then I become highly suspicious. Most companies use professionals to write their emails, sending them all through rounds of review and usually correcting most, if not all, errors.

- Email asking for something that doesn't seem normal – Sometimes, phishing emails pressure you into doing something by invoking fear or by offering unbelievable awards. Most legitimate emails from companies people do business with don't send emails that try to scare. Also, I ask myself whether the requested action involves any personal information. If so, does that seem like something the company would legitimately want me to do over email? And, as always, if an offer seems too good to be true, it probably is.

- Use of fake links or URL shorteners – If an email has fake links, I don't trust it. If an email uses link shorteners, I get suspicious and investigate where that link really goes (using getlinkinfo.com). There are legitimate uses of link shorteners and redirected links (marketers do this to track which links the email recipient clicks on). But it can be an indication of a malicious email.

- All email attachments from companies – Most companies don't send email attachments. They are more likely to send you a link to a file. Attachments from large organizations are a red flag for me.

- Numerous email addresses in the "To:" field, not just mine – Scammers often send a message to multiple people in one email, and they may obscure their actions by using the "BCC:" field for your and other emails instead of the "To:" field. Suspect any email asking for any type of personal information, which isn't specifically directed to you.

Figure 4. Example of a phishing email with notes indicating the ways you can tell it is fake.

Take Extra Precautions on Public Wi-Fi

Most businesses that directly serve consumers, like hotels, restaurants, coffee shops, and retail shops, provide Wi-Fi for their customers. So even if you use a device that doesn't have a cellular connection, like many tablets and laptops, you're almost always close to a place that can give you access to the Internet via public Wi-Fi. While this is a great convenience, it's not without risk. The convenience and number of people using public Wi-Fi also make it an attractive target for cybercriminals. Here are some risks of using public Wi-Fi:

- Hackers can intercept your online activity – One of the common public Wi-Fi cyberattacks involves a cyber-criminal positioning themselves between you and the Internet services you connect to. This man-in-the-middle attack can lead to cybercriminals' intercepting login credentials, credit card information, emails, and more.
- Cybercriminals can put malware on your device – Depending on the security settings of the public Wi-Fi network and your device security settings, a hacker can use file-sharing protocols to inject malware. The malware could be a virus, ransomware, worm, or any other type. It probably won't do anything until it is executed. Hackers have ways of getting you to execute a file. One way is by hacking the public Wi-Fi access point to display a pop-up that makes you think you are setting up your Wi-Fi connection while you are actually giving permission for the malware to run on your system.
- You can potentially connect to a compromised Wi-Fi access point or an imposter – If a cybercriminal gains administrative access to an access point, they can intercept your online traffic even more easily than

when they stage a man-in-the-middle attack. They can also more easily place malware on your device. Another way hackers can perform these cyberattacks is by setting up a Wi-Fi network with the same or similar name as the public Wi-Fi. If you connect to their Wi-Fi access point, then you are susceptible to cyberattacks.

Many security experts advise against using public Wi-Fi altogether. I think this is a drastic step. Most public Wi-Fi hotspots are safe to use. And, you can be protected using public Wi-Fi if you take the following precautions:

- Use a VPN – I recommended using a VPN to limit how much of your activity is tracked on the Internet. A VPN can also protect you on public Wi-Fi by providing an extra layer of encryption on all your activities. When you use a VPN, hackers trying to employ a man-in-the-middle attack will have to decrypt the information they've stolen in order to use it, which takes more time, resources, and know-how than most hackers are able to spend.
- Turn off file-sharing services – It's unlikely that you want to share files with anyone else connected to the same public Wi-Fi as you, so you should turn off sharing. Leaving sharing on enables hackers to exploit your system with malware. You can turn off sharing in the control panel of both MacOS and Windows and even set sharing to automatically turn off when your device connects to specific networks.
- Stick to HTTPS sites – HTTPS is the secure and encrypted version of HTTP. It can protect you from

man-in-the-middle attacks. However, make sure to pay attention to any warning your browser may give, even about HTTPS sites. Some hackers will attempt to give you a fake/invalid SSL certificate in order to make an HTTPS site look trusted. Your browser should detect this, but you have to pay attention to the warning.

- Turn your Wi-Fi off – If you aren't actively using your Wi-Fi to connect to a network, go ahead and turn it off. Wi-Fi cards still transmit and receive some information even when they aren't connected to a network. Although the chances are small, it's possible for a cybercriminal to exploit your Wi-Fi even when you aren't connected to a network. As a bonus, you'll have better battery life!

- If your mobile device has antivirus software, turn it on – This is good general advice, but it is especially important if you connect to public Wi-Fi. Antivirus software can detect common pieces of malware on your system.

- Double-check whether you are about to connect to the right Wi-Fi network – Hackers sometimes use an access point with a legitimate-sounding Wi-Fi network name to trick users into connecting to it. Then they can proceed to monitor everything you do over the connection and place malware on your device. Double-check the Wi-Fi name and credentials with the business providing the public Wi-Fi.

In the Real World: All VPN Services Aren't Equal

I've recommended a VPN in multiple cases and for good reason. VPN services can effectively provide you with a high level of cybersecurity and protect your privacy. When you use a VPN service, you encrypt and reroute all the data you send over the Internet through the VPN's server(s). Take care to find a good VPN solution, as they aren't all equal in their services and protection. Let's walk through some elements you'll want to consider when choosing a VPN service.

What Protocols Does It Support?

A VPN protocol is the technology VPNs use to determine how they communicate with other devices as well as how they encrypt the communications. Different VPN protocols have different levels of security and speed. Also, some devices natively support different VPN protocols better than other devices, although you usually can use a third-party app to support any of the major protocols. Here is a brief overview of the primary VPN protocols you are likely to see:

- OpenVPN – OpenVPN is the most popular VPN protocol supported by VPN services. It has a good combination of speed and strong encryption. OpenVPN also works through most firewalls. For most people, I recommend using OpenVPN. If the VPN service you are looking into doesn't provide this protocol, you should look elsewhere.

- WireGuard – WireGuard is the newest of the VPN protocols and is built for speed. In many tests, it outperforms OpenVPN's speed. Being a newer protocol, it isn't as well supported or as available as other protocols, but it is definitely one to watch.

- PPTP – Point-to-Point Tunneling Protocol is technologically ancient, insecure, and slow. It should be avoided for VPN use.

- L2TP/IPsec – This protocol is secure and mature but very slow when compared with OpenVPN and WireGuard. It is fine to use especially if the speed of the connection isn't of utmost importance or OpenVPN isn't available. Also, unlike with OpenVPN, firewalls have an easy time blocking this VPN protocol. This means that it won't work on some networks.

- IKEv2/IPsec – IKEv2/IPsec is faster than L2TP/IPsec, but fewer providers support it. Like L2TP/IPsec, it is susceptible to being blocked by firewalls.

- SSTP – Secure Socket Tunneling Protocol is considered fast and secure. However, it isn't as fast as OpenVPN. If for some reason you can't use OpenVPN, this would be a fine choice.

Does It Have Bandwidth, Connection, or Other Restrictions?

If you plan to use the VPN for a lot of heavier bandwidth services like streaming video and gaming, you will want to avoid providers that have bandwidth (data) caps. Also, think about all the services you plan to use while using the VPN and make sure none of those services is blocked or restricted by the VPN provider. You may need to read the fine print and do some research to figure out whether the VPN provider you're interested in has any of these limitations.

Does It Log Your Activity?

Although most VPNs don't log your activity, some of them do. If you value your privacy, you should look for a VPN service that either doesn't log your activity or keeps your activity data for a very short period. Some services use short-term logs to make sure their service runs properly.

How Much Does It Cost?

You should always consider the costs. Some factors that may affect the cost include the number of simultaneous connections (e.g., how many devices will use the VPN at the same time) and the type of your subscription—monthly, annual, or a lifetime one. Many VPN providers offer a free trial so you can try the service before committing to it. Also, there are often sales and promotions that you can take advantage of.

Related to cost, another factor you may want to consider is the payment methods the VPN provider offers. If you want ultimate privacy, which some people who are concerned with political prosecution do, some providers accept cryptocurrency and even gift cards from major retailers, like Amazon, Best Buy, Target, and Walmart, as means of payment.

Does It Have a Kill Switch System?

Like many other services, VPNs occasionally have glitches and stop working properly or altogether. If a VPN connection fails, a kill switch stops the connection immediately. Why is this important? If the VPN fails and the connection keeps going, this connection can no longer be protected and encrypted, leaking the information you probably try to protect by using that VPN. Once a kill switch stops the connection, you can choose whether you want to continue without the protection of the VPN.

■ Protecting Your Smartphone

Smartphones have become an integral part of our lives. We use them for financial transactions, connecting with friends, social media, email, scheduling, and many other activities. Through these activities, we store a lot of sensitive data on our phones, including private messages, pictures, videos, and login credentials. Smartphones contain so much important data that I thought I would include some cybersecurity tips specific to smartphone usage.

Download Apps from Only Trusted Sources

If you use Android phones, try to stick with Google Play for your apps. If you use iPhones, use Apple's app store. Both of these companies constantly monitor the apps they provide for malware and vulnerabilities. They have strict rules on what apps they allow in their stores. If an app you want isn't available in one of these app stores, be sure to research whether the app and the place you are getting it from are trustworthy.

Keep Your Phone Software Updated

This is good advice for all your computers. I know that everyone hates updates. However, many of these updates contain fixes to known exploits that cybercriminals can use to compromise your phone. You want your phone to have the latest security fixes installed. This includes the apps that you use.

Keep Your Screen Locked

Make sure your phone is set to automatically lock after a couple of minutes of inactivity, and manually lock it whenever you don't use it. If someone takes your phone while it is unlocked, they most likely have the keys to your digital kingdom. They can access all the apps that don't require you to log in again, make phone calls, and respond to two-factor authentication requests—all without having to know anything about you or any passwords. They can't do this if your phone is locked!

Enable Remote Data Wiping

What should you do if you're sure you've lost your phone and don't think you'll find it, a hacker has compromised your phone, or it is in the hands of a thief? Wipe all the data on it. Make sure to set your phone up to give you this ability remotely.

Be Wary of Text Messages

Text messages are a common phishing medium for cyber-criminals. Some will pose as people you know. Some will threaten you with some false and unfavorable action if you don't comply. Others try to befriend you in the long game to get key information out of you. Be skeptical of all text messages and make sure they represent whom they say they do before you respond.

Take Precautions with Bluetooth

While Bluetooth is very convenient for wirelessly connecting to devices and transferring files, it can also be an easy way for hackers to get into your phone. Make sure you keep your device from being discoverable, and always turn off Bluetooth when you don't use it. Additionally, don't accept pairing requests from devices you don't recognize. This could be a hacker trying to gain access to your phone.

The Best Ways to Protect Your Bank and Credit Card Information When Paying for Items

Paying for items by cash or check continues to be dwarfed by electronic payment methods. While this is great for convenience, it can also make payment systems and electronic ways of paying a larger target for cybercriminals.

Luckily, if you follow a few recommendations, your bank and credit card information will be well protected.

Best Practices for Online Payments

First, be sure you shop with reputable companies when paying for services online. You can use many of the techniques I detailed earlier such as the following:

- Making sure the site uses HTTPS instead of HTTP
- Paying attention to the browser notifications of security problems with the website
- Making sure the website actually represents a legitimate business
- Monitoring your payment accounts for fraudulent charges

In addition to verifying the validity of the site, you also need to decide which method you will use to pay. Let's discuss the pros and cons of the primary methods of paying for goods and services online.

PayPal, Venmo, Zelle, and Similar Services

These types of services work as the middle person between you and the party you purchase from. They store your credit card and/or bank account information and then send the payment to the store on your behalf, without revealing your bank or credit card information.

Pros:

- You keep your bank and credit card information private when making purchases.
- These companies utilize strong cybersecurity practices, because being trusted to make secure payments is crucial to their business models. By contrast, if you transact with your credit card directly with a shop, you rely on the shop's cybersecurity practices.

Cons:

- Sometimes, there are fees associated with transactions.
- A breach of the provider could result in multiple credit cards and/or bank accounts being compromised.
- Some loyalty/reward programs don't give you credit for purchases made on your credit card through these services.

Credit Cards

Purchasing online with a credit card is convenient and mostly safe if you shop at a reputable website.

Pros:

- Strong policies that allow you to get your money back when you are the victim of fraud. In the U.S., federal law states that if your card information—not your physical card—is stolen (as would be the case if your credit card information is compromised online), you're not liable for fraudulent charges. You may still encounter hassles getting charges corrected.

- You can earn loyalty points and rewards if your credit card is part of a program. These rewards may give you cash or other compensation opportunities just for using the card.

Cons:

- Giving a company your credit card information can be risky. A cybercriminal could intercept the information if the connection has been compromised. Additionally, the company's website could be compromised or its data centers breached, leaving your credit information in the hands of bad actors.
- Many companies store your information so you don't have to re-enter it again. While this can be convenient, it also means that your credit card information can be stolen if the company falls victim to a breach.

Debit Cards

A debit card looks like a credit card but works differently. When you use a debit card, the funds for the amount of your purchase are taken directly from your checking account, usually in real time. On the other hand, a credit card charges the amount against a line of credit, meaning you can pay the bill at a later date.

Pros:

- You enter debit cards into online payment systems the same way you enter credit cards, making them as convenient to use.

- There are no real cybersecurity advantages to using a debit card over a credit card. The primary financial advantage is that you can more easily control your spending with a debit card, because you can't spend money you don't have in the bank.

Cons:

- U.S. federal law limits your liability to US$50 if you report the fraudulent charges within 2 days but to US$500 if you report the fraudulent use within 60 days.
- Banks may also charge you overdraft fees if the card is used to draw more money than you have in your account, even if the charges are fraudulent.

Prepaid Cards

Prepaid cards work very similarly to debit cards. However, you can buy one from many different stores without having a bank account. You can usually buy cards worth a particular amount of money and use them like debit cards until the money runs out. Most of them allow you to add money to the account. Prepaid cards branded by Visa, Mastercard, or other card networks can be used anywhere those networks' cards are accepted.

Pros:

- You enter prepaid cards into online payment systems the same way you enter credit cards, making them as convenient to use.

- Like with debit cards, the primary financial advantage is that prepaid cards allow you to easily control your spending. Unlike with debit cards, you don't need a bank account to get a prepaid card. Additionally, unlike with credit cards, you don't need to have any minimum credit record level.
- You can't lose more money than is left on the card at the time it is compromised.

Cons:

- These cards don't have the same U.S. federal fraud protections as credit and debit cards do. However, card networks often work with consumers to give them their money back, provided the fraud or the lost card is reported in a timely manner. To gain this protection, card networks require users to register their cards, as opposed to buying and using them anonymously.

Overall, if you take the proper protections detailed earlier in this section, especially around verifying that the online store you shop with is legitimate, you will most likely be okay using any of these payment methods. However, you should avoid using prepaid cards and debit cards online if you have other options, because you're more liable for fraudulent charges when you use prepaid cards and debit cards than when you use credit cards.

PayPal, Venmo, and similar services are great to use if you are sure you either don't need loyalty/reward points for your purchases or know you'll get them anyway. These services can help reduce the number of places where you allow others to see your credit card and debit card information.

Whichever method you choose, I recommend not saving your PayPal, credit card, or debit card information with an online retailer. It may be inconvenient to re-enter your information each time. However, if the company is breached, your financial data won't be in the hands of cybercriminals.

Best Practices for In-Store Payments

While it's clear that you need to worry about cybersecurity when making online purchases, it may not be so clear that it's just as important for in-store payments. Unless you use cash, at least some of your payment information is transmitted and/or stored on payment networks and devices. Here are some good in-store payment practices you should follow when not using cash, checks, or gift cards to limit your susceptibility to cyberattacks.

Use a Digital Wallet
(Google Pay, Apple Pay, and Similar Services)

Services like Google Pay and Apple Pay allow you to make in-store purchases fast and securely using your mobile phone or smartwatch instead of a physical credit card. Using a compatible phone, you simply unlock the phone (make sure your phone has a lock screen set up!) and tap a payment terminal to pay. The payments are charged to a credit card you have registered for these services.

These services are more secure than using a credit card directly for the following reasons:

- Your actual credit card number is never sent. Payments are made using virtual credit card numbers and not your real credit card number. This protects you from fraudulent merchants and security breaches because you never give the retailer a chance to store your credit card number.
- You have to unlock your phone, using a fingerprint, face ID, password, or pin code, to be able to pay. This is an extra layer of security. In contrast, many stores don't require ID and/or a signature when you use a credit card. If someone steals your phone, they still have to be able to unlock it. And, you can track your phone. You can't track a credit card.

These services can be used with compatible debit and credit cards. You can store multiple credit cards and choose which one you want to use at any time.

Use Credit Cards with EMV Chip Technology

Most debit and credit cards feature embedded EMV (which stands for Europay, Mastercard, and Visa) chips. EMV chips transmit data similarly to the way data is transmitted when a card is swiped. However, an EMV-enabled card transaction is more secure because each payment transaction has its own unique code, which makes stealing data and counterfeiting chips much more difficult than when plain magnetic strip cards are used.

Most cards in the U.S. use chip-and-signature capabilities. This means that the cardholder signs to approve the transaction. Outside the U.S., the more secure chip-and-PIN transactions are more common. In these transactions, the card user must also know the card's associated PIN to complete the payment.

Some EMV cards can be used for contactless payments. When a card is used this way, you tap it to the payment terminal in the same way you would use Apple Pay or Google Pay. However, there's no need to unlock a phone when you pay in this manner.

Best Practices for Peer-to-Peer Payments

Have you ever gone to a restaurant with a group and forgot to put the meals on separate checks? Have you ever had coffee with a friend and accidentally left your wallet at home? How about having a night on the town and winding up in a place that accepts only cash, but you're the only one in your group that didn't bring any? These types of things happen all the time. The great thing about friends and family is that they are happy to cover you. However, you probably feel obligated to pay them back.

Peer-to-peer (or P2P) services make sending money directly to others painless. You can use them for tasks like splitting restaurant checks and pooling money to pay the rent. P2P services accomplish this by linking directly to your bank accounts and/or credit card accounts to send money to another user's account. They work very similarly to some online payment services mentioned earlier, except money is sent to an individual instead of a company. In fact, many of those same providers (e.g., PayPal, Zelle, and Venmo) also can make P2P payments. Google Pay, Apple Pay, Samsung Pay, and other digital wallets can also make payments directly to friends, family, and acquaintances.

While using these apps is great and much easier than counting up cash from different individuals at restaurant tables, they are still susceptible to fraud. Some common scams you should be aware of are as follows:

- Seller scams – A seller pretends to have some item you want and wants payment via a P2P app. You pay, but you never receive the item and the seller disappears.
- Buyer scams – How does a buyer who sends you money scam you? One way is that they somehow reverse or cancel the transaction shortly after receiving the goods.
- Mule scams – Someone sends you money and then asks you to send some of that money to another person, allowing you to keep some of the money. Why would they do this, and how are you being scammed? The scammer is most likely using you to launder money and just made you a party to illegal activity.

These scams aren't unique to P2P apps, but P2P apps are more susceptible to them because of the speed they can transfer money with and the relative lack of protections most of the services have because they aren't built for commercial transactions. To protect yourself from being victimized, take the following precautions when using these services:

- Always use some type of multi-factor authentication for payment apps (e.g., PIN or face unlock).
- Make sure your P2P apps are up to date. You don't want to miss any security updates to these kinds of apps.
- Favor linking credit cards instead of debit cards to P2P apps. As detailed earlier in this book, credit cards provide a higher level of fraud protection.
- **Never send money to anyone you haven't met in person. I can't emphasize this point enough.**
- Always confirm the contact information (email, mobile number, username, etc.) of the person you send money to.
- Don't use P2P apps for business. Most apps prohibit commercial payments except in explicit circumstances (usually, stores that have been approved by the app). Some apps, like PayPal, can be used for personal and commercial purposes, but you should properly identify the type of transaction when making it. Different rules, protections, and fees apply to different types of transactions.

I encourage you to think of money sent via P2P services just as you think of cash: You have instant access to it, and it's easy to give to someone but very hard to recover if it is given to someone by mistake. Be careful.

In the Real World: Watch Out for Card Skimming and Shimming

Card skimming is a thief's practice of putting a device on a card reader, usually a gas pump or ATM, to intercept and copy the magnetic stripe information from credit cards as they are slid through the compromised card reader. This gives the cybercriminal a copy of a customer's credit card number and other information that can include the card expiration date, the cardholder's name, and the card verification value (CVV). This information is usually sold on the black market or used to make counterfeit cards. Similar fraud can be perpetrated against other types of cards with magnetic stripes, like gift cards and hotel key cards.

One example of credit card skimming at gas pumps occurred from 2018 to 2020. Five men from Las Vegas installed card skimmers at gas pump terminals in Las Vegas, Reno, and various cities in southern California. During that time, they compromised thousands of credit and debit card numbers and recoded the data onto counterfeit cards. They then made multiple ATM withdrawals and purchases using the stolen credit card information.[6]

---

[6] "Five Men Indicted for Using Skimming Devices on Gas Pumps in Nevada and Southern California to Steal Customers' Credit Card Information," United States Department of Justice, accessed August 23, 2022, https://www.justice.gov/usao-nv/pr/five-men-indicted-using-skimming-devices-gas-pumps-nevada-and-southern-california-steal.

Card skimming has decreased in effectiveness due to the use of EMV (chip) cards. Many retailers, gas pumps, and ATMs have moved to supporting and favoring EMV card readers over magnetic strips. In reaction to this shift in technology, thieves have added card shimming to their fraud toolkit. Fraudsters insert what's called a "shim" into the EMV card reader, which allows them to copy the EMV card information. Although they can't use that information to create another chip card, they can use it to make a corresponding magnetic stripe card that can be used at retailers that don't require EMV cards. And, of course, they can sell this same information on the black market.

Before you use an ATM or gas station card reader, check for signs of tampering. Things to look for include the following:

- Anything looking out of place, such as mismatched colors, misaligned graphics, etc. If something doesn't look right, don't use that terminal.
- If you're at a bank or some place with multiple ATMs side by side, see whether one of them looks different from the other. If you spot some obvious differences, don't use either ATM and report your findings to the bank. The same goes for gas station pay terminals.
- You can also try pushing on the card readers a little bit. If it feels flimsy or like pieces are moving, that's another sign of tampering, as ATMs and gas station terminals are usually solidly constructed.

If you are ultra-paranoid about these machines, you can go to a bank teller or inside a gas station to complete your transaction in a more secure manner.

What I Do: Never Use Checks Unless Necessary

I don't write checks anymore unless there is absolutely no other way to make a payment. Between bill pay services, P2P payment services, mobile payment terminals, digital wallets, and credit and debit cards, I almost never need to. I go years without writing a check.

Although the primary reason I don't write checks is convenience, there are cybersecurity-related reasons as well. Checks contain lots of information that fraudsters love: your full name, your address, your bank name, your bank routing number, your bank account number, and your signature. Some merchants even require you to put your driver's license number on checks. Fraudsters don't even have to work for this information, as it is all there in plain sight.

With this data, thieves can make payments online using the account and routing numbers and thus taking money right out of your bank account. One common fraud activity is to use this information to buy prepaid credit cards. This information can also be used for identity theft, account takeover, and making fraudulent checks.

When you write a check, it passes through the hands of countless individuals from the merchant to the merchant's bank and then back to your bank. That's a lot of opportunities for fraud. One thing a person has to do to have all that information is pull out a smartphone and take a picture of the check.

The other downside of using checks is that when the account it represents is compromised, it's your money that's missing from your bank account (like a debit card), not the bank's money (like a credit card). In the United States, checking account holders have only two business days after receiving their bank statement to report fraudulent transactions; otherwise, they may be liable for up to US$500.

 ## What to Do If You Suspect You're the Victim of Fraud

It's hard to always follow best practices to protect yourself from fraud. Even if you are extremely careful and disciplined, you can still be the victim of fraud. We don't control all the systems that have our data. This point was reinforced when Equifax, a credit bureau that receives our personal data from financial institutions and other companies, was breached. If you have any type of credit, the credit bureaus will have your data.

How do you know whether you've been defrauded? Here are some signs:

- Unfamiliar credit card charges and bank withdrawals
- New lines of credit or requests for lines of credit on your credit report
- Denials for lines of credit you never applied for
- Calls from debt collectors regarding debt you are unfamiliar with—Watch out! This could also be a phishing attempt.
- Receiving a breach notification for a company you do business with
- Not getting mail you think you should be getting
- Receiving packages from stores that you didn't buy from (Cybercriminals may be using your accounts but occasionally forgetting to change the default shipping address.)
- Compromised online accounts or suspicious login attempts accessing your accounts

In addition to implementing the cybersecurity practices recommended in this section, you should also be prepared to act when you suspect you are the victim of fraud. If you learn that a corporate breach has potentially leaked your data, hackers have compromised a website that you use, you simply lost your credit card, or suspect your data was breached in any way, you should take the following steps to protect yourself.

Check and Monitor Your Credit Record

In the U.S., the three credit-reporting bureaus will each give you one free credit report each year, which you can get from AnnualCreditReport.com. You can also request a free credit report if you believe your credit report may contain fraudulent information (e.g., someone has opened up a credit account using your identity).

Place a Fraud Alert on Your Credit

A fraud alert is a notice placed on your credit report, which alerts credit card companies and other organizations that extend credit that you may be the victim of identity theft or some other fraudulent activity. When companies check your record to see whether you qualify for credit and see this "red flag," they most likely will take extra steps to verify the identity of the person trying to open the new account. There are two different types of fraud alerts:

- One-year alert – These alerts can be requested by contacting the credit bureaus directly, and they last for a year.
- Seven-year alert – Also known as an extended fraud alert, the seven-year fraud alert requires filing a police report or a Federal Trade Commission identity theft report.

You need to file a fraud alert with only one credit bureau, and it will appear on credit reports for all three bureaus. You can remove a fraud alert at any time.

Freeze Your Credit

A credit freeze restricts access to your credit report. Creditors can't open a new credit account on your record while a freeze is in place, even if it's genuinely you applying for credit. This offers you protection from someone trying to use your identity to gain credit, but it can be an inconvenience if you want to open up a line of credit. Fortunately, you can temporarily lift a credit freeze when applying for credit. In the U.S., all three credit bureaus are required to offer credit freezes free of charge. They last until you lift the freeze.

Note that you should request your credit be frozen with all three credit bureaus separately for the best protection. Different credit issuers contact different bureaus to check your credit. If you leave one unfrozen, anyone who uses the unfrozen credit bureau may still issue new credit. Credit freezes stay on your account until you lift them.

You may hear the terms *credit lock* and *credit freeze* used interchangeably. They offer similar protections but aren't the same. They both prevent creditors from accessing your credit report. However, credit freezes are mandated by the U.S. federal government to be free, whereas credit bureaus can charge for credit locks. Credit freezes must follow government regulations, whereas credit locks aren't governed by law. Additionally, credit bureaus typically make locking and unlocking your credit report easy to do in real time via an app.

Change Your Passwords

If you suspect you are a victim of fraud because you believe one of your accounts has been compromised, you should change the password to that account. Also, if you reuse that password with any other accounts, you need to change those account passwords as well. When you do change them, make sure the passwords are unique!

Monitor Your Financial Accounts

Cybercriminals are often financially motivated. They frequently target financial accounts with attacks because that's where the money is. If you think you may be a victim, monitor the charges and debits on all your bank and credit card accounts for any activity that looks unfamiliar. Inform your financial institution of any suspicious activity.

If You Know You're a Victim of Fraud

If you *know* you're the victim of fraud, you should take the following steps in addition to the recommendations in the previous section:

- Documenting what was taken, when, and how (if you know) – You should make lists of any money lost, fraudulent charges on credit cards, etc., so you can accurately report the theft to the authorities, financial institutions, and insurance companies.
- Checking your computer for malware – This is especially important to do if you aren't sure how cybercriminals accessed your accounts.
- Contacting the institution(s) affected by the fraud – You may need to close some accounts and open new ones.
- Reporting the fraud to the authorities – There are multiple agencies that handle different types of fraud.

At a minimum, report the fraud to the local police and the FTC. You'll need a police and/or FTC report for insurance claims and for extended fraud alerts. You can find more agencies to report the fraud to at USA.gov.[7]

- Disputing fraudulent transactions – You'll need to contact the fraud departments of the companies that service your compromised account and tell them each charge or debit that is fraudulent so that you aren't liable for the costs.
- Starting to repair your credit – If an identity thief has opened up credit accounts in your name or otherwise harmed your credit, you'll need to contact the credit bureaus and dispute the inaccurate information. The FTC provides information about the ways to dispute inaccurate information with each of the credit bureaus.[8]

 # What I Do: Keeping My Credit Frozen

Many companies that have some of my personal information have suffered data breaches. More companies with my data may have been compromised, but they haven't been, or never will be, aware of the breach. For this reason, I've decided to assume that my personal information that can be used for fraud is out there in cyberspace. To

---

7   https://www.usa.gov/stop-scams-frauds.
8   "Disputing Errors on Your Credit Reports," Federal Trade Commission Consumer Advice, accessed August 23, 2022, https://consumer.ftc.gov/articles/disputing-errors-your-credit-reports.

combat this, I keep my credit accounts frozen all the time. I unfreeze them only when I apply for a credit account. This way, even if someone tries to open a fraudulent account in my name, they'll be unsuccessful.

■ Key Takeaways

- ☐ Taking steps to protect yourself from cyberattacks and data breaches can make a big difference. Best practices for protecting yourself include the following:
  - ☐ Using unique and strong passwords for all accounts
  - ☐ Using multi-factor authentication
  - ☐ Setting appropriate privacy settings on all social media accounts
  - ☐ Limiting the personal information you share on social media
  - ☐ "Friending" only the people you know, on social media platforms
  - ☐ Limiting the number of third-party apps that have access to your social media data
- ☐ There are many ways that you are tracked on the Internet, including the following:
  - ☐ Your IP address
  - ☐ Your location
  - ☐ Tracking IDs that websites associate with you
  - ☐ Signing in to accounts
- ☐ You can limit how much you are tracked on the Internet by doing the following:
  - ☐ Turning on the "Do not track" request in your browser

- ☐ Disabling cookies in your browser
- ☐ Using Internet-tracking-blocker software
- ☐ Disabling location services on your phone
- ☐ Using search engines that don't track you
- ☐ Using a VPN when you connect to the Internet

☐ You can protect yourself from phishing and other social engineering attacks by doing the following:
  - ☐ Always being suspicious of unsolicited phone calls, visits, and emails asking for sensitive information
  - ☐ Making sure that private information requested by authorized organizations is absolutely needed before giving it out
  - ☐ Not providing personal or financial information in an email
  - ☐ Not submitting sensitive information to any website unless you've verified the site's identity and security
  - ☐ Taking advantage of anti-phishing features offered by your email clients and web browsers
  - ☐ Verifying that emails come from where they say they come
  - ☐ Limiting the information you post about yourself on social media

☐ Take the following precautions to protect yourself when using public Wi-Fi:
  - ☐ Use a VPN.
  - ☐ Turn off file-sharing services.
  - ☐ Stick to using HTTPS sites instead of HTTP sites.
  - ☐ Turn off your Wi-Fi when it's not in use.
  - ☐ Double-check that you're about to connect to the right network.

- ☐ You can protect your smartphone from hacking by doing the following:
  - ☐ Downloading apps from only trusted sources
  - ☐ Keeping your phone software updated
  - ☐ Keeping your screen locked when the phone isn't in use
  - ☐ Enabling remote data wiping
  - ☐ Being skeptical of text messages asking for sensitive or personal information
  - ☐ Turning off Bluetooth when it's not in use
- ☐ The best ways to protect yourself when making online payments include the following:
  - ☐ Making sure the websites you frequent use HTTPS instead of HTTP
  - ☐ Paying attention to browser notifications of security problems with a website
  - ☐ Making sure the website represents a legitimate business
  - ☐ Monitoring your payment accounts for fraudulent charges
- ☐ Avoid using debit cards when making payments online or in stores if possible.
- ☐ Avoid using checks to make payments.
- ☐ EMV chip credit/debit card transactions are more secure than transactions made with cards using magnetic stripes.
- ☐ When making peer-to-peer payments, protect yourself by doing the following:
  - ☐ Using multi-factor authentication with your P2P apps
  - ☐ Keeping your P2P apps up to date

- ☐ Never sending money to anyone you haven't met in person
- ☐ Always confirming the contact information of the person you're about to send money to

☐ If you suspect you're a victim of fraud, take the following steps:
  - ☐ Check and monitor your credit record.
  - ☐ Place a fraud alert on your credit record.
  - ☐ Freeze your credit.
  - ☐ Monitor your financial accounts.

☐ If you *know* you're the victim of fraud, take these additional steps:
  - ☐ Document what was taken.
  - ☐ Check your computer for malware.
  - ☐ Report the fraud to the appropriate companies and authorities.

Part 3

Protecting Your Home Network

The Importance of Protecting Your Home Network

Private family pictures and photographs. Sensitive financial information. Important software and devices that you and your family count on every day. If someone breaches your home network, they can compromise all these things. Bad actors are constantly trying to penetrate and compromise your network, steal your data, and co-opt your computers for malicious intent.

Not a day goes by without hackers' probing your network, trying to exploit vulnerabilities. This may sound like hyperbole, but it isn't. The firewall logs for my home router and my business websites show multiple scans and attempted break-ins every day. Luckily, most of them are unsophisticated and easily thwarted. The point, however, remains. Everyone should take their home network security very seriously. A compromised home network can result in identity theft, loss of important data, invasion of privacy and more, costing you time, money, and happiness.

Every home network should be designed and built with security in mind. The good news is that there are plenty of ways to block hackers and protect your home network. In this section, we discuss basic, intermediate, and advanced steps you can take to protect your home network. We also discuss secure ways to remotely connect to your network.

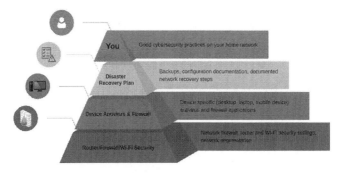

Figure 5. Network security pyramid noting some techniques and tools covered in this section

■ Basic Network Security Tasks

These basic network security tasks should be the minimum that you implement. They can be done easily in 10 minutes or less and don't require much technical knowledge. There are no excuses for not implementing these!

Keep Your Router and Other Network Device Firmware Up to Date

Your router (and the firewall in it) is your primary defense against hackers penetrating your network. New vulnerabilities are discovered all the time, and you want to make sure that your router has the latest protections. Periodically check to see whether your router has an available firmware update and keep your router up to date. Many routers will notify you of a firmware update. If your router no longer receives updates, you should consider replacing it, as it may be too old.

Similarly, you need to keep the firmware up to date on a Wi-Fi access point, a managed switch, Wi-Fi extenders, etc. Cybersecurity experts discover new vulnerabilities frequently, and the best way to protect your network is to keep the devices running your network up to date.

Keep the Client Devices Connected to Your Network Up to Date

Another common way hackers compromise your home network is through security vulnerabilities in the devices on your network. This includes PCs, laptops, mobile phones, smart TVs, surveillance cameras, and more. You can better protect your network by keeping the software and firmware on all your home network clients up to date as well. I know that everyone hates Windows updates, but they make your home network safer!

Keep Your Antivirus/Firewall Programs Up to Date

First, make sure your computers run an antivirus program. While your router firewall is your primary defense for your network, a strong antivirus and firewall program running on your computer is the primary defense for your computer. Most malware comes from sites and emails (usually phishing attempts) users interact with, not from hackers getting into your network. Protect the computer from yourself by making sure it has the latest protections your firewall and antivirus program provide.

Make Sure You Have Properly Configured Router Settings

At its core, a router is a device that takes your Internet connection and makes it available to all the devices on your home network. However, today's routers do much more than that. They hand out and manage the Internet Protocol (IP) addresses of all the devices on your home network so that those devices can talk to each other. They act as the first line of defense against hackers getting into your home network, by providing a firewall. Most routers also provide a Wi-Fi network for your home. It's extremely important to properly configure your router's security settings.

Log in to your router and check the following:

- Remote access is disabled. You should restrict the ability to log in and change your router settings outside your network. You want to be able to configure your router from your home network only (or even from specific computers only, but that's a more advanced topic).
- Your firewall is enabled. This should be the default, but you'll want to make sure!
- You have a strong password for logging into your router. Change the username if you can.

Change Your Home Wi-Fi Password(s)

Please tell me your Wi-Fi password isn't the default (and that you have one and have security turned on for your Wi-Fi network). Implement a strong password for your

Wi-Fi network and change it every so often, especially if you have neighbors that are in its range. There's a resource for how to implement strong passwords in the appendix of this book.

In the Real World: Even Brand-New Routers Need to Be Updated

Most consumers don't realize that many devices bought in stores ship with vulnerable firmware. Even routers you buy on Amazon are subject to this issue. CyberNews researchers recently found numerous flaws in a very popular TP-Link router sold by Amazon.[9] Most flaws are fixed in current versions of the router firmware. However sometimes, new routers are shipped running old versions of the firmware. Owners of the routers must update the firmware to fix these vulnerabilities; many routers don't update their firmware automatically.

The firmware security vulnerabilities enable hackers to easily compromise the router and gain access to the owner's home network. Here are some things hackers can do with control of your router:

- Intercept your web traffic and steal your usernames and passwords to any site, leading to identity theft

---

[9] Edvardas Mikalauskas, "'Amazon's Choice' Best-Selling TP-Link Router Ships with Vulnerable Firmware," CyberNews, accessed August 23, 2022, https://cybernews.com/security/amazon-tp-link-router-ships-with-vulnerable-firmware/.

- Install malware on the computers in your home network, including ransomware
- Make your router and the computers in your network part of a botnet group that mines cryptocurrency or attacks another network
- Compromise your video cameras to spy on you

There are more things a hacker can do if they take control of your router. Don't expect your router or other network devices to update their own firmware. Protect yourself by keeping your firmware updated, even in devices you just bought.

 # Intermediate Network Security Tasks

These intermediate network security tasks take a little more time to implement and even some research. They are more than worth the time for the extra security they provide.

Encrypt Your Drives

This is especially important for mobile devices like laptops, tablets, and mobile phones. If these are lost or stolen, thieves can easily access their drive without knowing the login information for your device by extracting the drive and connecting it to their device. Encrypting your drives makes it much more difficult for thieves to access your sensitive data, even if they have physical access to your device. If encrypting your entire hard drive seems too drastic, or like too much work, you can encrypt just the sensitive files you want to protect.

Set Up a Guest Network

If you don't have a guest network, you may find yourself in a situation where you have guests over and have to give them your password so they can access your network. This gives your guests not only your password, which may be sensitive and used for different accounts (again, you shouldn't reuse passwords), but also access to all your networked devices (printers, file shares, PCs, etc.). Sure, you probably trust the people who have your password, but do you completely trust that all the software and apps they use are free of malware that can compromise the devices on your network? You shouldn't. A proper guest network allows you to set a separate and shareable password for your guests. It also protects your private computer resources from being compromised by guests. Many routers and access points make configuring a guest network simple. If yours does, it's worth learning how to configure your guest network. If not, consider purchasing a router or access point that has the feature.

Set Up Regular Backups

Although not a direct protection against a network breach or computer infection, having a backup strategy can save you from catastrophic loss of data if there is a breach, or even if hard drives or computers fail. It can also help you restore your systems in case they are exposed to data corruption or ransomware. Here are a few options for backing up your systems.

Local backups

The easiest and quickest strategy is to set up a local backup somewhere in your house. This can be as simple as occasionally copying all your important files to a separate directory or hard drive on your computer. A step up would be to buy an external hard drive to store a backup on. One more step up would be to back up your files to a network-attached storage (NAS) machine (e.g., from Synology or QNAP). With some spare hard drives and low-powered computers, you can also pretty easily build your own NAS or turn your desktop PC into a NAS.

You can combine different types of local backups for better reliability and redundancy. For example, you could do the following:

• Storing all documents you want to back up on a NAS – Then you can use an external hard disk to back up the NAS. Some NAS devices have ports for external hard disks designed just for this scenario and can automate the backups.
• Backing up files to a separate directory/disk on your computer and then regularly creating a secondary backup on an external hard drive – This gives you backup redundancy.

If you are going to use a local backup strategy, I highly recommend that you use a NAS, an external hard drive, or a drive on a computer different from the computer that contains the files you are backing up. Having multiple copies on one computer as a backup is much riskier.

Back up documents to the cloud

Cloud storage for consumers and businesses has become a very hot and competitive business. Many services offer free storage, such as OneDrive, iCloud, Dropbox, and Google Drive. These services allow you to pay for additional storage. You can install apps on your computers and mobile devices to automatically back up important files to these cloud accounts. You can also create and directly access your documents in the cloud. All these services have your data backed up and replicated in multiple locations to keep your data safe. If you want to back up many photos or large video files, these services can become expensive.

Remote backup

OneDrive, Dropbox, Google Drive, and similar services are geared towards mostly syncing your data rather than backing it up. Their primary goal is to keep your files synced across multiple machines and devices, thereby providing access anywhere. In contrast, remote backup systems are best if you're concerned about backing up large amounts of data and want a higher level of security. Cloud backup providers encrypt your files before storing them, which makes your data more secure because the provider doesn't have the key to decrypt your data. Popular cloud backup services include Backblaze, SpiderOak, and IDrive. All these solutions come with software you can install on your

PC(s), and they schedule automated backups so you don't even have to think about it. Some of these solutions have apps that will back up your mobile devices too!

Alternatively, you could set up a remote server at a friend's house for remote backup, but that may require more work than it's worth!

Combining backup strategies

The more copies of your data, the less risk of data loss. A popular backup technique is the 3-2-1 backup strategy, which stands for the following:

- Three (3) copies of your data
- Two (2) local copies on two different devices (original and backup)
- One (1) offsite backup

This means combining the first strategy in this section (local backups) with one of the other strategies (backing up documents in the cloud or doing remote backup). For example, you could have a process that backs up to your NAS frequently and then performs a daily remote backup. Some cloud backup services have direct integration with popular NAS providers to make this process even easier.

Make sure you automate whatever strategy or strategies you decide to implement. Reliable backups are critical, and having to remember to back up a file is unreliable. There are apps and software available to automate backing up locally, with a cloud-syncing service, or remotely. Also, occasionally restore backups to ensure that your backup will work when you need it to.

What I Do: Backing Up My Important Files

I employ the 3-2-1 strategy. I have a NAS, and each night I back up all valuable documents, photos, videos, and other important files to a machine that is separate from my NAS. SpiderOak is the cloud backup service I use to remotely back up my NAS. All computers in my house have access to the NAS. My family knows that their important files are backed up locally and remotely every night.

One added benefit of using SpiderOak is that they keep copies of previous versions of files. If I haven't kept an old version of a file, I can find it in my cloud backup. This doesn't take up much extra storage space because of SpiderOak's deduplication (they store the changes to a file instead of a new backup each time). They also have a mobile app and web interface that allow me to access my backup files from anywhere.

Advanced Network Security Tasks

These tasks may take a significant amount of research and planning. Many of these concepts go beyond the basic use of routers and antivirus software. Take the time to learn how to implement these tasks to take your home network security to the next level.

Network Segmentation

If your IoT devices run on the same Wi-Fi network as all your other devices, they probably have access to the rest of your network. Unless you've done something explicitly to limit their access (e.g., VLAN, access control lists, a separate IoT Wi-Fi network), they are probably members of your network like any other device.

You may be asking why IoT devices need to be segregated from the rest of the network. The answer is that IoT devices have been hacked en masse. Lightbulbs, switches, thermostats, refrigerators, network cameras, and many more IoT devices have been hacked. Some have been compromised to attack other people and companies; some have been used to attack the device owners. IoT devices have revealed the network owner's Wi-Fi passwords.

IoT devices aren't known for having the best security features, and they are usually always connected and accessible from the Internet. Once these devices are compromised, they can be used to probe and attack other devices on your network. Sensitive personal information stored on your computer could be compromised. This is why you want to protect the rest of your network from these devices.

Segregating your IoT devices can be a complicated affair. Some ways of doing it involve modifying routing tables and setting up separate subnets. But nowadays, newer routers and access points have features where you can set up a network just for these types of devices, which secures your other network devices from them. This works very similarly to a guest network. You just end up putting your IoT devices on a separate network. When you look for a new router or AP, look for this function. Yes, we live in a world where we need to protect ourselves from lightbulbs and thermostats!

Monitoring for Unknown and New Devices

Do you know all the devices that should be on your network? Do you occasionally check your network to see whether unknown devices have connected? Ideally, your router allows you to monitor the devices connected to your network. To have your router alert you when new devices connect to your network would be even better. Most routers don't have that function, but you can use software that scans your network for new devices and sends alerts. There are free and paid options for whatever operating system you run.

Centralize Your Logs and Monitor for Breaches

You can do a lot more than monitoring what devices are on your network. Most people have many devices that interact with their home network. Some devices, like personal computers, routers, switches, and access points, log their activities. By examining these logs, you can detect all kinds of security breaches. However, all these devices produce a lot of logs to monitor. Going to each machine and application and inspecting the logs would take a lot of time. Fortunately, you can put log monitoring for security breaches on autopilot by centralizing your logs and using a log-analyzing tool—e.g., Graylog (which I use), Elasticsearch, ELK, and Splunk. What can you do and monitor with these tools?

Failed login detection

Windows event logs and syslogs contain records of authentication failures (such as entering a bad password). With centralized logging, you can set up an alert that emails you whenever there are too many (three is too many for me) unsuccessful authentication attempts in a minute. Authentication failures can indicate that someone is trying to break into your computer. So, alerts for these events are a good line of defense.

Notification of new machines on your network

If you assign all devices on your network an IP address, then you can be notified whenever an IP you haven't mapped joins your network. That way, you know when anyone new connects to your network.

Notification of users connecting to your guest Wi-Fi

Users who connect to guest W-Fi aren't usually already mapped to an IP. Your access point or router probably logs when users connect to your Wi-Fi networks, and you can set up your log analyzer to alert you whenever someone connects to your guest Wi-Fi. This is to make sure someone isn't mooching off your Wi-Fi unexpectedly.

Ability to search for particular events

Sometimes, things go wonky on a network or just happen, and you have no idea why. Often, you can successfully troubleshoot by looking through the logs. You can search through helpful logs to understand why applications have crashed or PCs have rebooted and to investigate unusual traffic in your network.

Set up a dashboard with key security metrics

You can set up a dashboard that quickly allows you to monitor key security metrics. For example, I have a dashboard showing me the number of times someone logs in to each machine and a graph of login failures. All this information is filterable by IP address and presented in charts that I can drill down into. For kicks, I also keep a histogram of how many security-related messages are in all the aggregated logs. It's a ton!

Malware Prevention at Network Level

You can process incoming Internet traffic for your home network and block malware and known hacker and hacking attempts. This is another feature that some higher-end routers and router software have, like pfSense. They are usually referred to as an intrusion protection system (IPS) or intrusion detection system (IDS). The easiest way to go about it is to buy a router that has these features or a dedicated firewall security device.

■ Have a Disaster Recovery Plan

One often-overlooked part of home network security is having the ability to recover from a network failure or a hack that compromises your network. You can take all the steps above and still get hacked. There are no foolproof solutions, just ways to make hacks less likely. For this reason, you want to be able to recover from a hack. A disaster recovery plan will help get your home network back up and running smoothly. A good network disaster recovery plan includes the following:

1. **The ability to detect outages or other disaster effects as quickly as possible.**
   As discussed in the Advanced Network Security Tasks section, monitoring your network is key to detecting breaches as soon as possible. The sooner these things are detected, the less damage can be done to your network and the quicker you can recover.
2. **Alerts sent to the network administrator (probably you) so action can be taken.**
   Timely notifications of network problems are important as also discussed in the Advanced Network Security Tasks section. Again, the person responsible for maintaining the network should find out about problems as soon as possible to thwart and recover from threats.

3. **Documented steps to isolate affected systems so that damage can't spread.**

   Often, the first step in managing a network breach to limit damage is to isolate the affected parts of the network so that these parts can't infect or impact other parts of the network.

4. **Documented steps to repair and/or rebuild the affected systems so that full home network function can resume.**

   Once you've diagnosed and stopped the threat, the repair work can begin. Having the recovery steps documented makes this process easier.

A hallmark of good disaster recovery planning is documentation. Sometimes, it's hard to think clearly in a crisis, and being able to follow well-written documentation is critical to remaining calm. Good disaster documentation includes the following:

- Well-documented configurations of key network devices such as your router, managed switches, file servers, and access points.
- A network diagram of your home, which includes network device locations, IP addresses, hostnames, the way they are connected to your network, VLANs, etc.
- Any manual configuration steps needed before and after restoring configuration files to your key network devices.
- Locations of key configuration files and backup files, as well as the way to gain access to them.

What I Do: Securing My Home Network

My first line of defense is my pfSense firewall and router. pfSense is actively maintained, and I make sure to keep it up to date with new firmware. I've made certain that remote access to my router is disabled. I've also taken additional steps to ensure only a couple of computers on my LAN can access my router's user interface, for additional security.

Snort and pfBlocker are packages available with pfSense, which I use to further protect my network from bad actors. Snort detects known intrusion signatures—telltale signs showing a system is being attacked—and blocks hackers trying to access my network. pfBlocker takes a different approach by reading regularly updated lists of known computers of hackers and other bad actors and blocking them from accessing my network.

I have more computers in my house than most, because I repurpose old hardware into file servers, multimedia distribution systems, virtualization hosts, etc. Every single one of these machines runs a firewall with rules to block other devices in my house from accessing popular network services (e.g., web connections, file and printer sharing, remote desktop, etc.). These rules are customized for each machine. My file server obviously allows most computers to access its files, and my web servers allow HTTP/ HTTPS connections. By default, however, my firewall rules are set up to block all my IoT devices from accessing anything unless I write in an exception. All my computers run Linux, and I use the UFW firewall software to accomplish this.

For additional Wi-Fi security, my home is separated into three Wi-Fi networks: home, guest, and IoT. Each Wi-Fi network has a unique identifying name. Computers on my home network have access to all other computers on my network, and security is a bit laxer. Computers on my guest network cannot access any other computer on my network and are also restricted from hogging all the bandwidth on my Wi-Fi. Computers on my IoT network are restricted from accessing most computers on my home network, with some exceptions. For instance, my security cameras need to save their video to my surveillance system hard drive, so they have access to that machine. My home automation controller (Home Assistant) needs to control many of my IoT devices, so they are permitted to access each other.

I put in an additional restriction for my security cameras. I use firewall rules in pfSense to block them from accessing the Internet. This way, hackers cannot look at the video from my cameras, and my cameras can send video not to the Internet but to my home network only. I can view my cameras while being away from home by connecting to my home network VPN (more on that later).

Graylog is the software package I use to centralize all the logs on my network. I have all the system logs from each computer, my router, and my access points sent to my Graylog service for processing and storage. Graylog is set up to alert me when unknown computers join my network (wired or wireless), when there are too many failed login attempts to any machine, and even when there are power outages (it receives information from my uninterruptible power supply). Additionally, from one interface I can search through the logs of all my machines when I try to hunt down a problem or an intrusion.

How to Perform a Security Audit on Your Home Network

Security audits are a regular part of doing business for IT departments in companies. Some industries have regulations requiring them to perform periodic security audits. And yet the same isn't true at home, of course. Most people never actually test the security of their home network. Here are a few things you should do at least once a year to audit your home network:

- **Run a network scan to determine all the devices connected to your network.** Make sure you recognize all the devices on your network. If you log and set up alerts as to when new devices join your network, you'll always know and won't need to do this scan. Nmap is my favorite tool for doing these types of scans, and there are many Nmap-based tools freely available for Linux, Windows, and MacOS.
- **Review your firewall and port-forwarding settings on your router.** These settings greatly affect the way people outside your network can access it. Make sure you know why all the firewall rules are there and what they do. Review your port-forwarding settings and

make sure you still need them. Port-forwarding settings allow users' computers in private networks to connect to computers in other networks. The fewer entries you allow into your network, the more secure it is.

- **Test for rogue Wi-Fi access points.** A rogue access point allows for a Wi-Fi connection to your network, which you haven't installed or set up. You'd probably find one of these when running a network scan. Additionally, some wireless routers and access points have the ability to scan your network for rogue access points.

- **Perform a penetration test.** The only way to know for sure whether your home network is secure is to see how it holds up to attempts to compromise it. Penetration tests (often referred to as "pen testing") use tools that can simulate standard attacks on your network to see how well your protections hold up. IT professionals often contract with a security firm to perform pen testing, but the costs are usually higher than what home network administrators would pay. Fortunately, there are tools out there that you can learn on your own to start doing pen testing and vulnerability scanning, including Metasploit, Wireshark, Hashcat, and Hydra. These tools take some time to learn, but they are worth it.

Remotely Connecting to Your Home Network Securely

Accessing the resources on your home network remotely can be convenient. Maybe you want to access a file that is only on one of your computer's hard drives. Maybe you want to see what's on a network camera, for security purposes.

One way to do this is to set up a secure remote desktop application. These run on a computer in your home and allow you to view and control that computer's desktop from another computer outside your home network. You can control that home computer pretty much as if you were sitting in front of it. Some popular options for remote desktop software are TeamViewer, Chrome Remote Desktop, Microsoft Remote Desktop, GoToMyPC, UltraVNC, and LogMeIn. Some of these are free and/or have free versions. If you decide to use one of these, make sure you pay attention to the ways of setting it up securely. You don't want to leave a low-security connection to a desktop on your network.

The biggest downside of using such remote desktop option is your having to leave a desktop running so that you can connect to it. Also, that desktop should not be in use by anyone else when you connect to it remotely. Otherwise, you'll have two people trying to control the same desktop at the same time. These are a couple of reasons why I prefer to set up a VPN connection. A VPN doesn't require the use of a desktop environment on a computer on your home network. It works by giving any device you use, including laptops and mobile phones, direct access to your network. Essentially, it makes your device work as if it is on your network from anywhere in the world.

Many routers come with VPN capabilities and offer a simple set-up. Another simple way of setting up a VPN is to buy a network security appliance that does VPN connections. These are devices that connect to your network with the sole purpose of protecting you from threats like malware and hackers. These devices go beyond the security of most routers. While these devices can add peace of mind to your home network security, they can be difficult for the average home user to configure. Examples of these devices targeted for home users include the Firewalla, the Bitdefender BOX, and the Zyxel Next Generation VPN Firewall. Also, if you are technically inclined, you can install and run your own VPN server on a computer in your network instead of buying a solution.

Many VPN protocols exist, and they all have differences, including varying levels of security. The one I recommend is OpenVPN. It combines security and speed with flexibility and wide device support.

 ## What I Do: OpenVPN via pfSense

OpenVPN was a straightforward VPN choice for me, because I use pfSense as my router, and pfSense supports OpenVPN. I use OpenVPN connections securely on my mobile phone to control my smart home remotely, to view security cameras, and sometimes to print. I also use OpenVPN on my laptop to view internal resources (e.g., some of my websites, videos, and virtual machine hosts) and to securely connect to machines at my leisure. It works consistently, is plenty fast, and has become a feature I take for granted.

■ Key Takeaways

- ☐ Implement basic security steps, including the following:
  - ☐ Keep your router and other network device firmware up to date.
  - ☐ Keep your client devices (mobile phones, laptops, PCs, etc.) up to date.
  - ☐ Make sure you keep your antivirus/malware scanner software up to date.
  - ☐ Make sure you've properly configured basic router security settings.
  - ☐ Make sure you have strong home Wi-Fi passwords.
- ☐ Implement intermediate security steps, including the following:
  - ☐ Encrypt your PC and mobile device hard drives.
  - ☐ Set up a guest Wi-Fi network.
  - ☐ Set up regular backups of important files.
- ☐ Implement advanced security steps, including the following:
  - ☐ Segment the various parts of your network from other parts (e.g., IoT, guest devices, surveillance cameras, etc.).
  - ☐ Monitor your home network for unknown devices.

☐ Centralize your computer logs, and monitor for security and failure events.

☐ Create a disaster recovery plan for your network.

☐ (If desired) securely connect to your home network remotely by using remote desktop software and/or a VPN.

Part 4

Special Considerations for Older People and Children

Good cybersecurity practices are especially important for older adults and children. Cybercriminals specifically target these two populations, and in some cases, they target them at a higher rate. Cybercrimes robbed Americans over 50 of nearly US$3 billion in 2021, which is a 62 percent increase from 2020, according to the FBI.[10] Children are often the target of identity theft. According to the Identity Theft Resource Center, 1.3 million children's records are stolen every year.[11]

Why Cybercriminals Target Older People

According to the FTC, almost 80 percent of scam victims are over the age of 65. Cybersecurity experts believe that seniors are targeted more because they take longer to adopt good cybercrime prevention tactics than younger adults do. For example, seniors are less likely than younger people to use multi-factor authentication when setting up banking accounts. They are also less likely to utilize any type of credit monitoring solution to alert them to potential fraud.

Seniors are also targeted because they have more wealth than younger populations do, making the cyberfraud

---

[10] Andy Markowitz, "Older Americans' Cybercrime Losses Soared to $3 Billion in 2021," AARP, accessed August 23, 2022, https://www.aarp.org/money/scams-fraud/info-2022/fbi-elder-fraud-report.html.

[11] "ITRC 2017 Identity Theft and Fraud Predictions," ITRC, accessed August 23, 2022, https://www.idtheftcenter.org/post/itrc-2017-identity-theft-and-fraud-predictions/.

payoff more worthwhile. Seniors are more likely to have amassed large "nest eggs" for retirement. They may also have more varied financial interests and accounts (insurance, retirement, brokerage, bank, and other accounts) that give cybercriminals more entry points for attack.

In addition, older adults are more trusting than younger generations. They are more likely to succumb to phishing scams via social media, emails, and phone calls because of their trust. These scams are also more effective against seniors because they have more family members and acquaintances than younger people do, whose private information can be used against them.

Lastly, seniors are also less likely to report that they've been the victim of a cybercrime. They are more likely to fear being shamed. Some may fear that their families could use their victimization as evidence they should no longer live alone or have complete control of their own money.

How Cybercriminals Target Older People

The ways in which cybercriminals target older people are just variations of the ways in which they target everyone. Senior citizens are more vulnerable to phishing scams, especially online and telephone scams. When targeting seniors, these phishing scams are likely to include too-good-to-be-true gifts and prizes, low-cost medications, or threats about medical or other benefits being cut off. Scam emails often send seniors to counterfeit sites that collect their credit card and other private information.

Another way in which older people are frequently targeted is through "confidence" fraud. Confidence fraud is when a cybercriminal poses as someone the victim trusts. Older adults are often targeted online, especially through social media. For example, the cybercriminal may pose as the victim's grandchild and get them to provide personal or financial information or to send money or gifts.

Even more disturbing, a cybercriminal may target the elderly, especially women who have been recently widowed, for a romance scam. When attacking seniors with romance schemes, cybercriminals create fake profiles and then use those profiles to first establish trusting relationships and then trick the victims into giving them money, gifts, access to accounts, and even into laundering money for them.

Identity theft is another common attack perpetrated against older adults. Although anyone can be the victim of identity theft, seniors are more often attacked through medical identity fraud, tax refund theft, and Social Security fraud:

- Medical identity fraud involves a criminal using someone's medical or insurance information to pay for services for themselves or to charge for services and pocket the money.

- Tax refund theft occurs when someone files a fraudulent tax return using someone else's Social Security number in order to get a refund.
- Social Security fraud often involves using a person's identity information to steal their Social Security payments.

How to Protect Older Adults

Naturally, the tips on the best practices for protecting oneself against cyberattacks apply to seniors as well. However, make sure you and the older adults in your life pay special attention to the following:

- Don't click on links in emails from people you don't know.
- Be skeptical of any messages asking for any type of personal information, even if they appear to come from someone you know.
- Ignore all unrecognized and unsolicited phone calls. If it's important, the caller will leave a message, and you can use that message to decide whether you should call back.
- Never reveal personal information by email or text. This includes credit card details, Social Security numbers, and other account information.
- Make sure to set appropriate privacy settings on all your social media accounts and to avoid posting sensitive information.

- Make sure that any website where you conduct financial or other sensitive transactions uses secure protocols (HTTPS) and that you've verified its legitimacy.
- Never be afraid to ask someone for help, and always reach out to trusted individuals and the authorities if you think you've been the victim of fraud.

In the Real World: Cybercriminals Targeted and Defrauded Older Adults of Over US$50 Million, Which They Then Laundered

From 2013 to 2020, a Ghana-based ring of cybercriminals targeted older adults through email spoofing and dating sites. The cybercriminals tricked them into wiring money and used their information to apply for government-funded coronavirus relief funds earmarked for small businesses affected by the pandemic.

Victims all over the United States were defrauded. Some were tricked into wiring money directly to the scammers by fake business emails. The scammers would spoof legitimate emails and impersonate employees of a victim's company to gain their trust.

Other victims were targeted with "romance scams," which targeted the victims via emails, texts, and online dating sites. The cybercriminals, using a fake identity, persuaded older single men and women into believing they were in a legitimate romantic relationship. After gaining the trust of the victims, they would use false pretenses to convince the victims to wire money to them.

In many of the scams, the victims were initially reluctant to come forward because of embarrassment. Some thought the chances of recovering their money and having the criminals prosecuted were too low to risk their reputational damage, which was one of the reasons these scams went on for as long as they did.

In the end, the scammers managed to fraudulently get and then launder over US$50 million.[12]

 ## Why and How Cybercriminals Target Children

Most fraud attacks against children involve identity theft, since children typically don't have a wealth of financial or other resources. However, cybercriminals can easily use youth Social Security numbers along with false names, ages, and addresses to apply for government benefits, lines of credit, and other financial accounts. Additionally, children's credit records are typically a blank slate, making

---

[12] "Six Defendants Arrested in Multiple States for Laundering Proceeds from Fraud Schemes Targeting Victims across the United States Perpetrated by Ghana-Based Criminal Enterprise," United States Department of Justice, accessed August 23, 2022, https://www.justice.gov/usao-sdny/pr/six-defendants-arrested-multiple-states-laundering-proceeds-fraud-schemes-targeting.

them easier to use than the bad credit records some adults have.

Another reason cybercriminals target children is because their data is easy to access. Kids tend to be significantly less cautious online than their parents. Children, especially younger children, are also more trusting than adults. They are more likely to post private details on social media, download and use fake and fraudulent gaming apps, and reveal private details through in-game chats.

Children are also targeted by cybercriminals because it takes their parents a long time to notice that their children are the victim of identity theft. Parents rarely, if ever, check their childrens' credit ratings. It's not uncommon for children not to realize they've been the victim of identity theft until they become adults and try to open up financial accounts of their own.

How to Protect Children

The best cybersecurity practices that apply to everyone apply to children as well. Much like with older adults, however, there are particular steps you should take to protect your children:

- Check your child's credit reports annually. If you see any unexpected information, you can take action to protect your child's credit record and identity.
- Consider freezing your child's credit reports. It's unlikely your children will need a line of credit until

they are adults. When the child reaches legal age, they can unfreeze their own account.

- Protect your child's Social Security number. Don't share your child's Social Security number with anyone or any organization that doesn't have a good reason to have it. Always ask why an organization needs your child's Social Security number and whether you can proceed without giving it.

- Avoid sharing too much information on social media. Parents love to share pictures and brag about their children's accomplishments online. However, be careful with what you share. Thieves mine these posts for birthdays, answers to security questions (like "Where did you go to elementary school?"), and other personal information. If you want to share this type of information, limit whom you share it with by using appropriate social media privacy settings.

- Monitor your child's social media and other online activity. It's best to insist that you have access to your child's social media posts to monitor what they post. You should also consider using fake names for your child's account to protect their identity. This can be a sensitive subject. I recommend explaining what can happen on social media and why you are concerned. Make sure children know the types of information they should never disclose, such as their address, phone number, or birthdate.

- Teach your children good cybersecurity practices and follow them yourself. Arm your children with the tools and techniques to protect themselves. Good cybersecurity practices will serve them for a lifetime.

What I Do: Protecting My Children from Cybercriminals

To protect our children from cybercriminals, my wife and I have taken the following steps:

- We don't use full first names on social media unless we share information with friends and family only. And, we don't post many pictures or share a lot of information about our kids.
- We continually educate our children about safely using social media and playing online games. We talk to them about being careful with the information they post and share, being careful about conversing with people in direct messages, and not using their real names in public online games and forums.
- Additionally, I monitor their online activities. Every so often, I scan what they post, talk to them about how they play and interact in online games, and check what apps they have installed on their phones.

Key Takeaways

- ☐ Older adults and children are specifically targeted by cybercriminals.
  - ☐ Older adults are targeted because they have worse cybersecurity practices, possess more wealth, and are more trusting than younger people.
  - ☐ Children are targeted because they have worse cybersecurity practices, and fraud against children takes longer to detect.

- ☐ Cybersecurity education with a focus on anti-phishing practices helps protect older adults.
- ☐ Teaching children good cybersecurity practices, monitoring and/or freezing their credit records, and reducing the personal information posted about them online—all protect them.

Part 5

The Future of Cybersecurity

Technology is constantly evolving. That's why it's important to consider what cybersecurity will look like in the future so you can be prepared to take advantage of new ways of protecting yourself from new and existing cyberthreats. Let's go over some of the ways cybersecurity may change over the next 10 years.

 ## Our Services and Data Will Continue to Move into the Cloud

This is a shift we already see happening. Companies will continue to use the cloud to provide increasing levels of service to more people easier, faster, and usually at a cost saving. Unfortunately, this also means more of our data will be in cloud systems and thus beyond our control. This may lead to even more data breaches.

Also, increasingly, the currency that the world trades in is data. Information about consumers (1) shapes product features and (2) drives advertising and numerous decisions that organizations and governments make. That means companies will be developing new ways of collecting and monetizing data. Cyberthieves will find that data is even more lucrative and more abundant, and thus we'll have more cyberattacks.

As individuals, we can protect against this by being selective about the companies we do business with and the data we provide them. We should always stay vigilant about monitoring our credit records and financial and other accounts. And, as always, don't reuse passwords!

While I truly believe that more and more services will move into the cloud, I think we'll start to also see an increase in peer-to-peer services and technologies in the next 10 years. We may have alternatives to cloud services that utilize blockchain and related technologies to provide us with more privacy and security. This may be a really positive cybersecurity development.

We'll See an Increase in Biometrics and Other Ways of Authenticating

Society hates having to remember so many passwords. Many people, from renowned cybersecurity expert Roger Grimes to Microsoft founder Bill Gates, have been predicting the death of the password for decades. Despite those prognostications, today we have more passwords than ever. They are convenient, and everyone knows how to use them.

However, we do have better ways of authenticating ourselves. Biometrics—ways of using a unique physical or behavioral characteristic to identify and authenticate ourselves—have been further permeating mainstream usage. Some examples include face unlock capabilities in mobile devices, voice matches in smart speakers, and fingerprint readers. We also have multi-factor authentication hardware keys.

These more convenient and often more secure methods of authentication will grow in the future, but they will probably still have a password or PIN fallback. Passwords aren't going away. But it's time to get comfortable with other methods of logging in to systems.

Our Homes Will Contain More Devices That Can Be Hacked

More and more household electronics have been gaining the "smart" label. In addition to the smart TVs, smart speakers, smart plugs, smart bulbs, and other almost ubiquitous smart tech we have in our homes, smart refrigerators, smart water heaters, smart stoves, smart coffee makers, smart washers and dryers, etc., have been becoming more available and more normal. While this opens up exciting possibilities for the smart home, it also means devices in your home can be hacked. It will continue to be important to follow good home network security practices.

Quantum Computing Will Require Updates to Our Cryptography Algorithms

Quantum computing is based on the principles of quantum theory. Unlike conventional computing, which breaks down computational components into bits, quantum computers use quantum bits, also known as qubits. Quantum computing will have a significant impact on cryptography, which is the backbone of the current encryption methods used to keep much of our data safe, because it will be able to break many current encryption methods very quickly. To combat this, organizations are already working on quantum-resistant cryptography.

Artificial Intelligence Will Play a Larger Role in Cybersecurity Threats and Protection

Artificial intelligence (AI) can already be used to detect security intrusion attempts. In the future, it will be used in more security products, especially ones powered by the cloud, to detect and combat cyberattacks at companies and in your home. Unfortunately, artificial intelligence will also be used more often by cybercriminals to find weaknesses and penetrate systems too. The cybersecurity future we are looking at is that of bot versus bot.

Cyberattacks Will Be a New Face of War

Cyberattacks conducted and sanctioned by governments already exist. Outside of war, governments use cyberattacks for data gathering, disabling infrastructure systems, and spreading misinformation. During conflicts, cyberattacks are primarily used to disrupt communications and other military systems.

State-sponsored cyberattacks more frequently target non-government agencies. Many now target businesses or end up hurting businesses as collateral damage. At some point in the future, cyberattacks themselves may be considered acts of war. Cyberattacks have already damaged the operations of ports, power grids, and even nuclear centrifuges. Despite all that, the age of cyberwarfare is just in its infancy.

This means there will probably be an increase in well-funded and powerful groups of hackers attacking businesses and services that you may use. Although you can't directly make a company more secure, you can take appropriate steps to lessen the impact of data breaches, such as using strong unique passwords and monitoring your accounts.

■ Key Takeaways

- [ ] The data we store in cloud services will increase in the future, emphasizing the need for everyone to implement good cybersecurity practices.
- [ ] Biometrics and other forms of authentication will grow in use, but we'll still have plenty of passwords.
- [ ] We'll have more devices in our home network than ever in the future, increasing the importance of good home network security.
- [ ] Quantum computing could compromise current encryption methods, necessitating the adoption of quantum-safe encryptions.
- [ ] Artificial intelligence will help increase the capabilities of defending against cyberattacks and cybercriminals.
- [ ] Cyberattacks will increasingly become part of warfare, and the businesses we use as well as our data may fall victim to them. This is another reason to improve your cybersecurity habits.

Appendix A – Checklists

Best Social Media Cybersecurity Practices

☐ Double-check your social media privacy settings.

☐ Turn off location access in your social media apps.

☐ Make sure location data is removed from pictures that you post online.

☐ Check your "friends" or "connections" for people you don't know and remove them.

☐ Beware of fake profiles (impersonation).

☐ Don't friend or connect with people you don't know.

☐ Limit the personal information in your profiles.

☐ Check which third-party apps have access to your social media data. Remove access for any that you don't recognize or you don't think need access.

☐ Refrain from answering viral sets of questions about yourself in social media posts.

☐ Don't take personality quizzes and surveys unless you know how your data will be used and are comfortable with it.

☐ Limit the pictures and personal information that you post about your young children and grandchildren.

Best Password Practices

☐ Use a password manager.
☐ Use multi-factor authentication whenever it is available.
☐ Don't reuse passwords.
☐ Make your passwords at least 15 characters long.
☐ Use a hard-to-guess but easy-to-remember phrase as a password.
☐ Pick security questions only you know the answers to.
☐ Change passwords immediately after finding out any site you use has been breached.
☐ Don't tell others your passwords.

Best Public Wi-Fi Cybersecurity Practices

☐ Use a VPN.
☐ Turn off file-sharing services.
☐ Use only HTTPS sites with a valid SSL certificate.
☐ Turn off Bluetooth and Wi-Fi when you don't use them.
☐ If your mobile device has antivirus, turn it on.
☐ Make sure you are connected to the right public Wi-Fi network.

Best Financial Transaction Cybersecurity Practices

- ☐ Make sure to use only HTTPS-enabled sites.
- ☐ Pay attention to browser notifications of website security problems.
- ☐ Make sure the website actually represents a legitimate business.
- ☐ Monitor your accounts for fraudulent withdrawals and charges.
- ☐ Try to use digital wallets (e.g., Google Pay, Apple Pay, PayPal) or credit cards for payments instead of debit cards.
- ☐ Don't save your credit/debit card numbers with merchants when making payments.
- ☐ Prefer using EMV credit card readers to swiping magnetic strips.
- ☐ Never use P2P payment services (e.g., Venmo, PayPal, and Zelle) to send payments to anyone you haven't met in person.
- ☐ Don't use P2P apps for business/commercial purchases.
- ☐ Use multi-factor authentication with all financial apps and accounts.
- ☐ Beware of card skimmers and shimmers, especially at gas stations and ATMs.
- ☐ Don't use checks.

Fraud Victim Checklist

☐ Document what was taken, when, and how.

☐ Report the fraud to the authorities.

☐ Dispute any fraudulent transactions.

☐ Check your computer for malware.

☐ Check and monitor your credit record.

☐ Place a fraud alert on your credit record.

☐ Consider freezing your credit.

☐ Change passwords or close compromised accounts.

☐ Monitor your financial accounts for suspicious withdrawals and charges.

☐ Start repairing your credit if necessary.

Home Network Security Checklist

☐ Your router firewall is turned on.

☐ Your router is less than five years old or still gets frequent updates.

☐ Your router firmware is up to date.

☐ You use WPA2 or WPA3 security with AES.

☐ You have a strong Wi-Fi password.

☐ You've changed your Wi-Fi password in the last year.

☐ You have a guest network.

☐ You've isolated your IoT devices.

☐ Your router web interface isn't accessible from the Internet.

☐ Your Wi-Fi network isn't set to the default name.

☐ You know all the devices on your home network, and monitor your home network for new devices.

☐ Your antivirus/malware software is up to date.

☐ You've encrypted the hard drives of your mobile devices (phones, tablets, laptops, etc.).

☐ You've centralized your computer logs, and monitor them for security and failure events.

☐ You regularly back up important files.

☐ You have a written disaster recovery plan for your home network in case of emergency.

Best Cybersecurity Practices for Protecting Your Children

- ☐ Protect your child's Social Security number.
- ☐ Monitor your child's credit report.
- ☐ Consider freezing your child's credit report.
- ☐ Avoid sharing too much information about your children on social media.
- ☐ Monitor your child's social media and other online activity.
- ☐ Teach your children good cybersecurity practices.
- ☐ Show your children that you adhere to good cybersecurity practices.

Appendix B – How to Set Recommended Facebook, Instagram, and Browser Privacy Settings

Here is how to set the Facebook, Instagram, and Chrome browser privacy settings I've mentioned earlier in this book.

 ## How to Set the Recommended Facebook Privacy Settings

Most Facebook privacy settings can be changed using only the web interface and aren't available using a mobile app.

Turn on Two-Factor Authentication

Although not strictly a privacy setting, two-factor authentication is important for guarding your Facebook account and the data it contains. Facebook supports multiple two-factor options. I recommend using a security key or an authenticator app. To turn on two-factor authentication, from a computer click your profile icon in the top right corner of the Facebook home page and go to Settings & privacy > Settings > Security and Login. On this screen, you'll see the Two-Factor Authentication setup section.

Restrict Tracking of Off-Facebook Activity

On a computer: Go to Settings & privacy > Settings > Your Facebook information > Off-Facebook activity.

From there, select "Clear previous activity." To prevent the data from being used for targeted ads going forward, select "Disconnect future activity."

Note that turning this function off disables the Facebook login tool, meaning you can no longer sign in to apps and websites, using your Facebook login credentials. An alternative is to go service by service and disable Off-Facebook activity for each service for which you don't need Facebook login.

Restrict Who Can See Your Posts

Facebook gives you the option to limit who can see each new video, photo, or status update post. However, you can set the default privacy setting for new posts and change old posts as well. On a computer, go to Settings & privacy > Privacy > "Who can see your future posts?" > Edit. Here, you can set the defaults for new posts and review and change who can see old posts.

Disable Third-Party Apps

You can choose which third-party apps have access to your account (and, consequently, which apps share information about you with Facebook). On a computer, go to Settings & privacy > Settings > Apps and Websites. Here, you'll see a list of apps that have access to your Facebook data. You can remove access completely or review and modify what the apps have access to.

Hide Your Location Data from Facebook

Facebook gets your location data from its app. On an Android or iPhone, you can disable location tracking, using the device's settings. However, Facebook may still use your mobile device's network information to get an approximation of your location.

On an iPhone: Go to the phone's Settings > Privacy > Location Services > Facebook. Then click either "While Using the App" or "Never."

Instructions for Android phones vary more by model and age of the device. On most Android phones, go to Settings > Location > App location permissions > Facebook > Select "Allow only while using the app" or "Deny."

Remove Your Facebook Profile from Google Searches

On a computer: Go to Settings > Privacy > "Do you want search engines outside of Facebook to link to your profile?" > Edit and remove the check mark next to "Allow search engines outside of Facebook to link to your profile."

Stop Facebook from Using Your Information for Advertising Targeting

On a computer: Go to Settings > Ads > Ad Settings. Here, you can tell Facebook what data it is allowed to use to target you with ads.

 # How to Set the Recommended Instagram Privacy Settings

Turn on Two-Factor Authentication

Although not strictly a privacy setting, two-factor authentication is important for guarding your Instagram account and the data it contains.

On the Instagram app: Go to your profile by clicking the icon on the bottom right > Open the menu in the top right > Settings > Security > Two-Factor Authentication > Tap the login method you want to use and follow the next instructions. Of the choices available, I recommend using an authentication app.

Make Your Posts Inaccessible to Strangers

On the Instagram app: Go to Settings > Privacy. Switch on the Private Account toggle.

Note, people who already follow you will still be able to see your posts after making this setting change.

Hide Your Location Data from Instagram

These instructions are the same as they are for Facebook.

On an iPhone: Go to the phone's Settings > Privacy > Location Services > Instagram. Then, click either "While Using the App" or "Never."

Instructions for Android phones vary more by model and age of the device. On most Android phones, go to the phone's Settings > Location > App location permissions > Instagram > Select "Allow only while using the app" or "Deny."

Limit the Ways Instagram Stories Can Be Shared

This setting allows you to stop others from sharing your Instagram stories with their followers.

On the Instagram app: Go to Settings > Privacy > Story. Under Sharing, switch off the toggles for "Allow sharing to story" and "Allow sharing to messages."

Limit Data Sharing with Third-Party Apps

On the Instagram app: Go to Settings > Security > Apps and Websites > Active. Select the desired app and press Remove.

Limit the Ways Instagram Can Recommend Your Account to Others

Oddly enough, this feature can't be set in the Instagram app.

On a browser: Log in to Instagram > Click on your profile picture in the top right corner of the screen to open the menu > Profile > Edit Profile > Uncheck the box for Similar Account Suggestions.

Disconnect Contact Syncing

On the Instagram app: Go to Settings > Account > Contacts Syncing. Turn off Connect contacts.

How to Set the Recommended Chrome Browser Privacy Settings

These instructions are specific to the Chrome web browser. However, you can find similar settings in other browsers.

Turn on "Do Not Track"

Select Settings under the three-dot menu on the top right of the browser. Then, select Privacy and Security > Cookies and other site data. From there, toggle on the option "Send a 'Do Not Track' request with your browsing traffic."

Limit Cookies

Go to Settings > Privacy and Security > Cookies and other site data. Here, you can limit what cookies you can receive and how long they last. I recommend blocking third-party cookies and clearing cookies when you close all windows.

Turn on Safe Browsing

Go to Settings > Privacy and Security > Security and select a Safe Browsing option. I recommend "Enhanced protection." If you are wary of sending data to Google, then choose the standard option.

Disable Location Tracking

Go to Settings > Privacy and Security > Site Settings. In the location-setting section, you can allow sites to ask for your location or block all sites from seeing your location. I recommend the latter setting.

Encrypt Your Sync Data

Go to Settings > You and Google > Sync and Google services. Choose to encrypt your synced data with a password.

Appendix C – Additional Resources

- **HomeTechHacker Blog** (https://hometechhacker. com/) – This is my personal blog where you can find many helpful articles about cybersecurity and improving your home network and smart home.
- **HomeTechHacker Shop** (https:// hometechhacker.com/shop/) – Here, I maintain an up-to-date list of recommended home network and smart home devices.
- **CNET Home Internet** (https://www.cnet.com/ home/internet/) – This site has an abundance of information and reviews of home network products.
- **AnnualCreditReport.Com** (https:// annualcreditreport.com) – This is the site authorized by U.S. federal law to help you get one free credit report a year from each bureau.
- **The Ambient** (https://www.the-ambient. com/) – This site has lots of up-to-date reviews on the latest home network products.
- **Digital Trends** (https://www.digitaltrends.com/ smart-home-reviews/) – Their home technology product reviews are thorough and entertaining.

- **The Hacker News** (https://thehackernews.com/) – The Hacker News features breaking cybersecurity news and up-to-date advice and information that can help you deal with data breaches and cyberattacks.
- **Infosecurity Magazine** (https://www.infosecurity-magazine.com/) – In addition to cybersecurity advice and information, Infosecurity Magazine offers free webinars, whitepapers, and virtual conferences.
- **Troy Hunt** (https://www.troyhunt.com/) – A cybersecurity thought leader, who travels the world speaking and training technology professionals. He also blogs about current cybersecurity trends and makes recommendations on how you should protect yourself.
- **Have I Been Pwned?** (https://haveibeenpwned.com/) – Run by Troy Hunt, this site monitors data breaches and the data contained in them. This site can tell you in real time whether your email or phone number has been found in data leaked via a breach. You can also sign up to be alerted when your data is part of a breach. Both of these services are free.
- **pfSense Documentation** (https://docs.netgate.com/pfsense/en/latest/) – I've been really happy with pfSense software running my router. It's free software with lots of documentation and features that can run on hardware of your choice. You can buy a router with pfSense preinstalled. This documentation will get you started.
- **SmallNetBuilder** (https://www.smallnetbuilder.com/) – SmallNetBuilder is a great site if you're looking to make your home network the best it

can be. It is filled with tutorials, reviews, and an extremely helpful forum for technical assistance.

- **ZDNet** (https://www.zdnet.com/) – It has tons of product reviews about everything home technology, including cybersecurity and home network products and services.

- **How to Create a Strong Password (and Remember It)** (https://www.howtogeek.com/195430/ how-to-create-a-strong-password-and-remember-it/) – This is a great resource for creating good passwords from How-To Geek.

Glossary

AES – AES (i.e., Advanced Encryption Standard) is a technology used to encrypt data and secure transmission of data between devices. Wi-Fi networks use AES to secure data transmission.

Authentication – The process of verifying that someone is who they claim to be.

Backdoor – In cybersecurity, a backdoor is a way to access a computer system or application, which doesn't use its intended methods of authentication (i.e., the frontdoor). A developer may create a backdoor so that an application or operating system can be accessed for troubleshooting or other purposes.

Bad Actor – A person or organization who is a threat and may attack technology systems and defraud people and organizations.

Biometrics – Unique physical characteristics, such as fingerprints or a retinal scan, that can be used to verify someone's identity (authentication).

Black Hat Hackers – Hackers with malicious intent. They try to compromise systems mainly for monetary gain, but also for ideological reasons. They use cyberattacks to hold computers hostage, access sensitive information, and destroy files.

Botnet – A network of hijacked computers infected with malware, which carry out various scams, cyberattacks, and other actions at the behest of the cybercriminals controlling them.

Card Shimming – When a thief inserts what's called a "shim" into the EMV card reader, which allows them to copy the EMV (chip) card information.

Card Skimming – When a thief puts a device on a card reader, usually at a gas pump or ATM, and intercepts and copies the magnetic stripe information from credit cards as they are slid through the compromised card reader.

Cat 5e, Cat 6, Cat 6a, Cat 7, Cat 8 – These are all different standards of Ethernet cable, which are the backbone of the wired network in your home. The higher the number, the later the Ethernet standard. The later the Ethernet standard, the faster speeds the cable will support over longer distances. If you are laying down new wire at the time of my writing this book, try to get at least Cat 6a, which can support a 10-Gigabit connection for 100 meters.

Cookie – A piece of data from a website stored within a browser, which can be retrieved at a later time. Websites use cookies to keep track of who you are and what activities you partake in when you visit a site.

Cryptocurrency – A digital currency in which transactions are verified and records are maintained by a decentralized system using cryptography rather than by a centralized authority, like banks and governments.

Cryptography – The study of communication techniques that allow a sender to securely transmit messages to intended recipients.

Cyberattack – An attempt by hackers to damage or infiltrate a computer system or network.

Cybercriminal – A person who uses and/or targets computer systems and networks while committing crimes.

Cyberfraud – A crime of using and/or targeting computer systems and networks that deceives or corrupts others for money, power, or some other motive. Personal and financial information are the common targets of cyberfraud.

Cybersecurity – The practice of protecting computer networks, devices, and data from unauthorized or criminal use. This book focuses on *personal* cybersecurity, which is the practices individuals and families should take to protect themselves from cybercriminals.

Dark Web – The part of the web accessible by only those with the proper anonymizing software, allowing its users and website operators to remain anonymous or untraceable.

Digital Wallet – Otherwise known as an electronic wallet, refers to software, an electronic device, or an online service that allows you to make financial transactions online.

DHCP – (i.e., Dynamic Host Control Protocol) is a network management protocol used to automate configuring device IP addresses. This allows each device to communicate with other devices easily. Devices can have IP addresses that aren't assigned by a DHCP server (static IP addresses), but these must be configured manually. As networks get larger, it's easier to manage IP addresses, using a DHCP server. Usually, your router functions as the DHCP server on your network.

DKIM – (i.e., DomainKeys Identified Mail) is an email authentication protocol designed to detect forged sender addresses in email (email spoofing).

DMARC – (i.e., Domain-based Message Authentication, Reporting, and Conformance) is an email authentication protocol that helps protect email senders and recipients from spam, spoofing, and phishing. DMARC, which uses DKIM and SPF, allows an organization to specify to email servers how to handle the unauthorized use of email domains.

DNS – (i.e., Domain Name System) is the Internet's system for converting domain names to IP addresses.

EMV – (i.e., Europay, Mastercard, and Visa) is a set of standards governing authentication technology for credit and debit cards utilizing an embedded chip.

Encryption – A way of securing digital data, using one or more mathematical techniques. Encrypted data must be decrypted in order to be understood.

Firewall – A network security device that monitors incoming and outgoing network traffic and decides which parts of that traffic to block from entering or exiting your network, based on a set of rules. It is primarily used to protect your network from threats coming from the Internet. A firewall can be a standalone device, but it is most often a function available in your router.

Gateway – A network device that connects two networks with different transmission protocols. In a home network setting, your gateway is most likely the modem or modem/router combo your ISP provides.

Gray Hat Hackers – These hackers look for vulnerabilities in computer systems without the permission of the owner. They usually inform the owner of a found vulnerability; sometimes, they require payment for the information needed to fix the issue.

Hacking – The attempt to exploit or damage a computer system or network.

IoT – (i.e., Internet of Things) is a collection of interconnected and interrelated devices that can communicate and transfer data over various networks without human interaction. It most commonly refers to any device that connects to the Internet. Examples include smart TVs, smart speakers, toys, wearables, smart appliances, and smart meters.

IP Address – (i.e., Internet Protocol address) is a numerically based label that uniquely identifies a device on a network.

ISP – (i.e., Internet Service Provider) is a company that provides Internet as a service to a home or business. These are often cable and other telecommunications companies like Comcast, CenturyLink, and Verizon.

LAN – (i.e., local area network) is a computer network that usually connects computers in a specific geographic location—a home, a school, or an office building.

MAC Address – (i.e., a media access control address) is a hexadecimal address assigned to network devices. MAC addresses are typically unique to a particular device and can be used to identify devices on a network and to assign devices unique IP addresses.

Malware – Short for "malicious software," it refers to software specifically designed to damage, disrupt, or gain unauthorized access to a computer system. Viruses, spyware, worms, and ransomware are all types of malware.

Man-in-the-Middle Attack – Occurs when the attacker is positioned between the two communicating computers or computer systems and intercepts the traffic to and from each computer or computer system.

Modem – Short for modulator-demodulator, it converts signals from one type of device to another type of device. One example is a cable modem, which converts signals from a coaxial cable (analog) to an Ethernet signal (digital) that routers typically use.

Multi-Factor Authentication – Describes security technologies and practices that require multiple methods of authentication in order to access a system.

NAT – (i.e., network address translation) allows a single device to act as an agent between the Internet and your local network. It enables private IP networks (like most home networks) to share a public IP address and Internet connection. A router usually implements NAT, allowing all the computers on your network to have a private IP address but appear as a single address when accessing Internet resources such as websites.

Network Penetration – When hackers search for and identify security vulnerabilities in your network or on the connected computers in your network. Hackers exploit these vulnerabilities to gain access to, and control of, your network devices and data.

Network Segmentation – An approach to network configuration that divides a local area network into multiple segments. This is usually done to securely isolate parts of the network from other parts and for performance reasons.

Penetration Testing – Also called pen testing, this is a method of testing used to identify vulnerabilities in network security. Penetration testing launches multiple controlled attacks against a network in order to see how well it holds up. The results of the test are used to bolster the network's defenses.

Phishing – These attacks trick users into revealing personal information, such as passwords and credit card numbers, through fraudulent solicitation, usually from an email or a website.

Qubits – A qubit, also known as a quantum bit, is quantum computing's counterpart to the binary digit in classic computers. It holds information that quantum computers use to do computations.

Quantum Computing – Computing based on the principles of quantum theory. Unlike conventional computing, which breaks down computational components into bits, quantum computers use quantum bits, also known as qubits. Quantum computers promise to be exponentially faster at most tasks than today's computers.

Router – This device forwards (or routes) packets of data between different networks. For instance, the router in your home routes packets coming from your ISP (WAN) to your private home network (LAN) and vice versa.

Smart Home – A home that provides some combination of comfort, energy efficiency, security, lighting, etc., aided by technology that allows these systems to be automated, integrated, and available for remote control.

Social Engineering – These attacks, sometimes referred to as human hacking, are attempts by hackers to trick people into giving them access, private information, or other valuables. These attacks can happen in person, by phone call, online, and via other types of interactions.

SPF – (i.e., Sender Policy Framework) is an email authentication method designed to detect forged sender addresses. Internet service providers use SPF records to verify that a mail server is authorized to send email for a specific domain.

Spoof – When someone, usually a cybercriminal, impersonates someone or something else's identity. For instance, sending a fake email that looks like it's from a sender (but, in fact, isn't) is an email spoof.

Switch – Also called a network switch, this is a device in a computer network, which connects multiple devices (e.g., computers, access points, printers, etc.).

Two-Factor Authentication – Also known as 2FA, this is a type of multi-factor authentication that requires only two methods.

VPN – (i.e., virtual private network) allows a device to communicate securely across a public network with a private network (such as your home network). VPNs work by encrypting the data that travels over the Internet between a device and the private network. VPNs can also be used to connect private networks securely over the Internet.

WAN – (i.e., wide area network) is a computer network that covers a large geographic region. WANs are similar to LANs but aren't limited to a single location and are usually larger.

White Hat Hackers – Sometimes referred to as "ethical hackers," white hat hackers are the antithesis of black hat hackers. They implement cyberattacks to find vulnerabilities that need fixing. They are often contracted by organizations to assess the security of a company's systems.

Wi-Fi – The name of a wireless networking technology that uses radio waves to provide high-speed network connections.

Wireless Access Point – This device connects to a router, switch, or hub via Ethernet and emits a Wi-Fi signal for connecting to your network. Wireless access points are used for extending a wireless network.

WLAN – (i.e., wireless local area network) is just a wireless version of a LAN, which is a computer network that usually connects computers in a specific geographic location—a home, a school, or an office building.

WPA – (i.e., Wi-Fi Protected Access) is a security standard used to protect Wi-Fi network access. The original WPA standard is considered insecure. All your devices should be using WPA2 or WPA3.

Zero-Day – This term refers to the fact that a vendor or developer has just learned of a flaw that others know about, meaning they have "zero days" to fix it. A zero-day attack is one in which hackers exploit a flaw before developers can address it.

About the Author

Best-selling author Marlon Buchanan is an IT Director by day and a home technology hacker (the good kind) by night. He has over 25 years of combined experience as an IT director, software developer, systems analyst, college instructor, and home technology consultant. He has a bachelor's degree in computer science and engineering from MIT and master's degrees in business administration and software engineering from Seattle University.

He has been automating things around his house since he was a kid. Now, his wife and kids get to enjoy the fruits of his smart home exploits. He is best known for his smart home, home networking, and cybersecurity articles on his blog HomeTechHacker.com, and his best-selling books *The Home Network Manual* and *The Smart Home Manual*.

Please sign up for his newsletter on his blog. You can also follow him on these social media channels:

- Twitter – Twitter.com/HomeTechHacker (@HomeTechHacker)
- Pinterest – Pinterest.com/HomeTechHacker
- Facebook – Facebook.com/HomeTechHacker

What Did You Think of *The Personal Cybersecurity Manual?*

First of all, thank you for purchasing *The Personal Cybersecurity Manual.* I know that you could have picked any number of books to read, but you picked this book, and for that I am extremely appreciative.

I hope that it has inspired you and helped improve your cybersecurity practices. If so, it would be really nice if you could share this book with your friends and family by posting about it on Twitter, Facebook, and Pinterest.

If you enjoyed this book and found some benefit to reading it, I'd love to hear from you. I hope that you can take the time to post a review on Amazon. Your feedback and support will help me greatly improve my writing craft for future projects.

I want you, the reader, to know that your review is very important and very appreciated.

I wish you all the best in protecting yourself from cybercriminals!